BELIEVE WHAT GOD SAID WORKBOOK AND REFLECTION JOURNAL

Genella Harper

Faith Pages Publishing

Atlanta, GA

Copyright Page

© 2024 by Faith Pages Publishing

All rights reserved. No part of this publication may be reproduced, distributed, or transmitted in any form or by any means, including photocopying, recording, or other electronic or mechanical methods, without the prior written permission of the publisher, except in the case of brief quotations embodied in critical reviews and certain other noncommercial uses permitted by copyright law.

Published by Faith Page Publishing

ISBN: 9798333378439

Printed in United States

Dedication

To all who seek to walk by faith and not by sight,
May this book inspire and strengthen your journey.
May you find courage in the stories of those who
Believed what God said and saw His promises fulfilled.
This work is dedicated to the relentless pursuit of faith,
And to the God who remains faithful through it all.

Table of Contents

PROLOGUE	**6**
INTRODUCTION	**8**
CHAPTER 1: THE FOUNDATION OF FAITH	**10**
REFLECTION AND APPLICATION: PROCESSING YOUR FAITH JOURNEY	**15**
REFLECTION AND APPLICATION: ENDURING FAITH	**22**
CHAPTER 2: HEARING GOD'S VOICE	**26**
REFLECTION AND APPLICATION: OVERCOMING CHALLENGES IN DISCERNING GOD'S VOICE	**30**
REFLECTION AND APPLICATION: PERSONAL TESTIMONIES WORKBOOK	**36**
CHAPTER 3: WALKING BY FAITH, NOT BY SIGHT	**43**
CHAPTER 4: STANDING FIRM IN THE STORM	**48**
REFLECTION AND APPLICATION: STANDING FIRM IN THE STORM	**52**
CHAPTER 5: THE NEHEMIAH PRINCIPLE	**55**
REFLECTION AND APPLICATION: THE NEHEMIAH PRINCIPLE	**57**
CHAPTER 6: OVERCOMING OPPOSITION	**61**
REFLECTION AND APPLICATION: DEALING WITH OPPOSITION AND CRITICISM	**65**
CHAPTER 7: THE POWER OF GOD'S PROMISES	**67**
REFLECTION AND APPLICATION: TRUSTING IN THE POWERS OF GOD	**69**
CHAPTER 8: FAITH IN ACTION	**73**

REFLECTION AND APPLICATION: FAITH IN ACTION 75

CHAPTER 9: THE REWARD OF FAITHFULNESS 77

REFLECTION AND APPLICATION: REMAINING FAITHFUL TO GOD 81

CONCLUSION 84

FREQUENTLY ASKED QUESTIONS 86

APPENDIX: ADDITIONAL RESOURCES FOR DEEPENING YOUR FAITH 88

Prologue

Faith is the foundation upon which our relationship with God is built. It is the assurance of things hoped for, the conviction of things not seen (Hebrews 11:1). Throughout the pages of the Bible, we encounter men and women who exemplified this kind of faith—individuals who trusted in God's promises, even when those promises seemed impossible. Their lives serve as powerful testimonies to the reliability and faithfulness of God.

In a world often characterized by uncertainty and doubt, the call to believe what God has said resonates more urgently than ever. The scriptures are filled with God's promises and assurances, yet walking by faith requires more than acknowledging these truths; it demands a heartfelt trust that translates into action, especially when circumstances seem contrary.

This book is a journey through the lives of those who have gone before us, who chose to stand firm on God's word despite overwhelming challenges. From Abraham's obedient departure to an unknown land to Mary's humble acceptance of God's plan, each story provides a unique perspective on what it means to live by faith.

1. **Abraham** believed God's promise of a great nation, stepping out in faith without knowing his destination (Genesis 12:1-4).
2. **Noah** built an ark in obedience to God's command, despite never having seen rain (Genesis 6:9-22).
3. **Ruth** trusted in God's providence and chose loyalty over convenience, leading her to a place of honor (Ruth 1:16-17).
4. **Daniel** maintained his integrity and faith, praying to God even under the threat of death (Daniel 6:10-23).
5. **Mary** accepted God's call to bear the Savior, demonstrating humility and submission (Luke 1:26-38).

These figures, and many others, showcase the transformative power of faith in God's word. They remind us that faith is not merely a passive belief but an active trust that propels us to move forward, even when the path is unclear.

As you delve into these stories, may you be encouraged to deepen your own faith. Reflect on the promises God has spoken into your life, and find the courage to believe and act upon them. For it is through walking by faith and not by sight that we truly experience the fullness of God's plans and purposes for us.

Welcome to a journey of faith—a journey that calls us to believe what God has said and to stand firm on His word, no matter the challenges we face. May this book inspire you to trust in the unwavering faithfulness of God and to live a life marked by steadfast faith.

Introduction

In our journey of faith, we often encounter challenges that test our resolve and belief in God's promises. Life's storms can be overwhelming, causing doubt and fear to creep into our hearts. However, it is during these trying times that our faith is most crucial. This book is a guide to walking by faith, standing firm on what God has told us to do, regardless of the circumstances or the opinions of others. It is a reminder that God's promises are sure, and His timing is perfect, even when we cannot see the full picture.

Faith is not just a passive belief but an active trust in God, demonstrated through our actions and decisions. It requires us to hold on to His word, even when the path ahead seems uncertain. Just as Abraham trusted God for a son and Job remained faithful amidst immense suffering, we too are called to trust in God's goodness and faithfulness. Their stories, along with many others in the Bible, serve as powerful examples of unwavering faith that we can draw strength from.

One of the most inspiring examples of steadfast faith is Nehemiah. Faced with the daunting task of rebuilding Jerusalem's walls amidst fierce opposition, Nehemiah remained focused on God's call. He did not let the threats and distractions deter him from his mission. Instead, he relied on prayer and God's guidance to overcome every obstacle. Nehemiah's determination to stay on the wall, despite the challenges, is a profound lesson for us. It teaches us the importance of staying true to God's purpose for our lives, regardless of the external pressures we face.

The Bible also assures us of the rewards that come from remaining faithful to God. Galatians 6:9 encourages us, saying, "Let us not become weary in doing good, for at the proper time we will reap a harvest if we do not give up." This promise is a beacon of hope, reminding us that our efforts and faithfulness are not in vain. God's rewards may come in various forms—spiritual growth, peace, joy, and even material blessings—but they are always worth the wait.

In this book, we will explore the power of faith through biblical stories and teachings. We will delve into the lives of individuals like Abraham, Job, Paul, and others who triumphed over adversity through unwavering faith. Their experiences will inspire and challenge us to trust God more deeply, even in the most turbulent situations. We will also discuss practical steps to live out our faith daily, from serving others to expressing love in our actions.

Moreover, we will examine the concept of God's timing and the importance of remaining patient. The story of Joseph, who endured years of hardship before seeing God's promise fulfilled, is a powerful testament to the fact that God's plans often unfold over long periods. His timing may not align with our expectations, but it is always perfect. As we wait on God, we learn valuable lessons in trust, obedience, and perseverance.

This book is more than just a collection of stories and teachings; it is a workbook designed to help you reflect and apply these lessons in your life. Each section includes thought-provoking questions and journal prompts to guide your personal journey of faith. By engaging with these exercises, you will deepen your understanding of God's word and strengthen your resolve to remain faithful, no matter the circumstances.

As we embark on this journey together, let us remember that faith is the foundation of our relationship with God. It is through faith that we experience His power, receive His promises, and grow spiritually. May this book inspire you to walk by faith, stand firm on God's word, and trust in His perfect timing. No matter what challenges you face, know that God is with you every step of the way, guiding and sustaining you.

Chapter 1: The Foundation of Faith

Faith is the cornerstone of our relationship with God. Let's look at the definition of a cornerstone. A cornerstone is traditionally the first stone set in the construction of a masonry foundation. It is important because all other stones will be set in reference to this stone, thus determining the position of the entire structure. In a broader sense, a cornerstone can also refer to something of fundamental importance that everything else depends on or is based on, such as a key principle or concept in an organization or system. Hebrews 11:1 tells us that "Now faith is confidence in what we hope for and assurance about what we do not see." It involves trusting Him completely, even when we can't see the full picture. This chapter explores the essence of faith, delving into what it means to have faith and how it impacts our lives. Romans 10:17 explains that "Consequently, faith comes from hearing the message, and the message is heard through the word about Christ."

Faith as the cornerstone and foundation of life is a powerful metaphor that conveys its fundamental role in shaping and guiding a person's beliefs, actions, and purpose. Just as a cornerstone is the first stone laid in a building, faith is often the first principle in a person's spiritual journey. It serves as the starting point that defines the alignment and direction of one's life, setting the stage for other virtues and beliefs. Without faith, other aspects of spirituality and morality can lack coherence and strength.

When faith is the cornerstone, it becomes the measure against which all other beliefs and actions are aligned. It provides a sense of stability and assurance, especially during challenging times. Faith enables individuals to persevere, to find meaning and hope amidst difficulties, and to trust in a higher purpose or plan. This unwavering trust acts as a stabilizing force, much like a cornerstone that holds a structure steady. The Bible underscores this idea in Ephesians 2:20, which states, "built on the foundation of the apostles and prophets, with Christ Jesus himself as the chief cornerstone." This highlights the fundamental role of faith in Christ as the basis for all other beliefs and practices.

Moreover, faith as the foundation implies that it undergirds everything else in a person's life. It supports the weight of other values and principles, giving them context and significance. For believers, faith in God provides the assurance that they are part of something greater than themselves, offering a sense of belonging and purpose. It influences decision-making, behavior, and interactions with others, promoting a life that is congruent with one's deepest convictions. Hebrews 11:1 emphasizes the essence of faith, saying, "Now faith is confidence in what we hope for and assurance about what we do not see." This verse reinforces the idea that faith provides a stable foundation, even when circumstances are uncertain.

In essence, faith being the cornerstone and foundation of life means that it is both the beginning and the support of one's spiritual and moral edifice. It is what everything else is built upon and aligned with, ensuring stability, coherence, and a sense of purpose throughout life's journey. This concept is further illustrated in Matthew 7:24-25, where Jesus teaches about the wise and foolish builders: "Therefore everyone who hears these words of mine and puts them into practice is like a wise man who built his house on the rock. The rain came down, the streams rose, and the winds blew and beat against that house; yet it did not fall, because it had its foundation on the rock." Here, faith in Christ's teachings is likened to a solid foundation that can withstand life's trials and tribulations.

Let's examine biblical examples of faith in action. These examples of faith in action provide powerful lessons and inspiration for believers. One of the most prominent examples is Abraham, who is often referred to as the "father of faith." His story, along with those of other key figures, illustrates profound trust in God despite seemingly impossible circumstances.

Abraham: The Father of Faith

Abraham's journey of faith is also marked by the promise of a son despite his and Sarah's advanced age. In Genesis 15:1-6, God reassures Abraham that he will have a biological heir, even though Abraham and Sarah were well beyond the typical childbearing years. Abraham believed God's promise, and his faith was credited to him as righteousness. This moment is pivotal because it illustrates that faith often involves believing in the seemingly impossible. Despite the natural impossibilities, Abraham trusted God's word, demonstrating that faith is not about our limitations but about God's limitless power and faithfulness.

Furthermore, the birth of Isaac itself is a testament to Abraham's enduring faith. In Genesis 21:1-7, we see the fulfillment of God's promise as Sarah gives birth to Isaac. This event highlights the joy and fulfillment that comes from trusting in God's promises. It wasn't just a victory for Abraham and Sarah but also a tangible proof of God's faithfulness and power. Through Isaac, the promise of numerous descendants began to take shape, laying the groundwork for the nation of Israel. Abraham's unwavering belief in God's word, despite the long wait and numerous obstacles, serves as an enduring example of faith and patience.

Abraham's interactions with God also include moments of intercession, demonstrating his deep relationship with the Creator. In Genesis 18:16-33, Abraham pleads with God to spare Sodom and Gomorrah if righteous people can be found within the cities. This passage reveals Abraham's faith in God's justice and mercy, as well as his boldness in approaching God with his concerns. It underscores the aspect of faith that involves not only trust and obedience but also a personal and dynamic relationship with God. Abraham's faith journey was multifaceted, encompassing obedience, belief in promises, intercession, and an intimate walk with God, making him a profound model of faith for believers throughout the ages.

Moses: Leading with Faith

Moses's faith journey is profoundly illustrated not only through his initial encounters with God but also in his ongoing leadership and intercession for the Israelites. After the dramatic escape through the Red Sea, Moses faces the daunting challenge of leading a large, often rebellious, group of people through the desert. In Exodus 16 and Numbers 11, we see Moses' faith as he intercedes for the people and trusts God to provide manna from heaven and quail to sustain them. These acts of provision demonstrate God's faithfulness and Moses's reliance on divine guidance and support. His leadership, underpinned by faith, ensures that the Israelites are sustained both physically and spiritually throughout their journey.

Moreover, Moses's intimate relationship with God is a cornerstone of his faith. In Exodus 33:11, it is said that the Lord spoke to Moses face to face, as one speaks to a friend. This unique relationship not only empowered Moses but also provided him with the strength to lead. Moses often spent time in God's presence, receiving the Ten Commandments on Mount Sinai (Exodus 20) and seeking guidance for leading the Israelites. His faith was deeply rooted in this personal connection with God, which allowed him to act with confidence and authority. Moses's example teaches us that faith grows through consistent and deep communication with God.

Another significant aspect of Moses's faith journey is his perseverance despite repeated challenges and opposition. Whether dealing with the grumbling and complaints of the Israelites (Exodus 17:1-7) or facing the rebellion of Korah (Numbers 16), Moses continuously turns to God for wisdom and strength. His resilience is a testament to unwavering faith in God's plan, even when human logic and circumstances seemed insurmountable. Through his life, Moses exemplifies that true faith involves enduring patience, steadfast trust, and an unwavering commitment to God's calling, regardless of the trials that come our way.

David: Faith in the Face of Giants

David's encounter with Goliath is a profound example of unwavering faith in the face of seemingly insurmountable odds. As the youngest son of Jesse, David was not a seasoned warrior but a shepherd boy. Yet, his faith in God was so strong that he volunteered to fight Goliath when the entire Israelite army was paralyzed with fear. David's confidence was not in his own ability but in God's power. In 1 Samuel 17:45, David boldly declares to Goliath, "You come to me with a sword and with a spear and with a javelin, but I come to you in the name of the Lord of hosts, the God of the armies of Israel, whom you have defied." This statement underscores his complete reliance on God for victory.

The significance of David's victory over Goliath extends beyond the battlefield. It marks the beginning of David's rise to prominence in Israel and showcases the impact of faith on one's destiny. By trusting in God, David not only defeated a giant but also demonstrated to the

Israelites the power of faith in action. His faith inspired others and set a powerful example for future generations. David's story reminds us that God can use anyone, regardless of their status or experience, to achieve great things when they place their trust in Him.

      Furthermore, David's faith journey did not end with his triumph over Goliath. Throughout his life, David faced numerous challenges, including being pursued by King Saul and dealing with personal failures. In each instance, David turned to God for guidance, forgiveness, and strength. Psalms, many of which were written by David, reflect his deep faith and dependence on God. Psalm 23, for example, portrays his trust in God's provision and protection: "The Lord is my shepherd; I shall not want." David's ongoing reliance on God, even in times of trouble, illustrates that faith is a continuous, enduring relationship with the Creator.

Reflection and Application: Processing Your Faith Journey

This section is designed to help you process what you have read and apply the lessons of faith from the lives of Abraham, Moses, and David to your own life. Use this workbook to reflect deeply, journal your thoughts, and identify areas where you need to exercise faith.

Reflect on Abraham's Faith

1. **Understanding Obedience**:

    a. **Question**: What was Abraham's initial act of faith, and why was it significant?

    b. **Reflection**: Reflect on a time when you had to step into the unknown, trusting that God had a plan for you

    c. **Journal Prompt**: Write about a moment in your life when you felt God calling you to take a step of faith. How did you respond? What were the outcomes?

2. Sacrifice and Trust:

    a. **Question**: How did Abraham's willingness to sacrifice Isaac demonstrate his ultimate trust in God

    b. **Reflection**: Think about a situation where you had to give up something important to you. How did this test your faith?

    c. **Journal Prompt**: Describe an instance when you had to trust God with something precious to you. What did you learn about faith and trust from this experience?

Reflect on Moses' Faith

1. **Courage in Leadership**:

    a. **Question**: What challenges did Moses face when God called him to lead the Israelites out of Egypt?

    b. **Reflection**: Consider a leadership role you have taken on. How did faith play a part in your ability to lead effectively?

    c. **Journal Prompt**: Write about a time when you felt inadequate for a task but chose to rely on God's strength and guidance. How did your faith help you overcome obstacles?

2. Perseverance through Trials:

    a. **Question**: How did Moses demonstrate perseverance and reliance on God in the wilderness?

    b. **Reflection**: Recall a period of difficulty in your life. How did your faith help you persevere?

    c. **Journal Prompt**: Reflect on a challenging time in your life when you had to rely on your faith to get through. What did you learn about God's faithfulness?

Reflect on David's Faith

1. Facing Giants:

    a. **Question**: What does David's victory over Goliath teach us about facing our own giants?

    b. **Reflection**: Identify a "giant" in your life that you are currently facing. How can faith help you confront and overcome this challenge?

    c. **Journal Prompt**: Describe a significant challenge you are facing right now. How can you apply the lessons from David's faith to your situation? What steps can you take to trust God more fully?

2. Confidence in God's Deliverance:

    a. **Question**: How did David's confidence in God's past deliverances strengthen his faith to face Goliath?

    b. **Reflection**: Think about past instances where God has delivered you or answered your prayers. How do these experiences bolster your faith for current challenges?

    c. **Journal Prompt**: Reflect on moments when you have seen God's hand at work in your life. How do these memories strengthen your faith in facing current or future obstacles?

Your Faith Journey

1. Current Situations:

    a. **Question**: What are some current situations in your life where you need to exercise faith?

b. **Reflection**: Identify specific areas where you are struggling to trust God completely.

c. **Journal Prompt**: Write about one or two situations you are currently facing where you need to exercise faith. What fears or doubts do you have? How can you remind yourself of God's promises and past faithfulness?

1. **Prayer and Commitment**:

    a. **Question**: How can prayer and reading God's Word strengthen your faith in these situations?

    b. **Reflection**: Consider the role of prayer and scripture in building and maintaining your faith.

    c. **Journal Prompt**: Commit to a plan for prayer and Bible study that will help you grow in faith. Write out a prayer, asking God for the strength and courage to trust Him more fully in the specific situations you are facing.

Use these reflections, questions, and journal prompts as tools to deepen your faith and apply the biblical lessons to your own life. Remember, faith is an ongoing journey, and each step you take in trust brings you closer to God's purpose and plan for you.

Enduring Faith: The Testament of Job's Resilience and Trust

Job, renowned for his unwavering faith in the midst of profound suffering, stands as a timeless example of spiritual resilience and trust in God's plan. In the ancient land of Uz, Job was esteemed not only for his wealth and stature but also for his unwavering devotion to God. Described as blameless, upright, and deeply reverent toward God, Job's integrity was beyond reproach. However, his faith would soon face an unprecedented test that would challenge even the strongest of believers.

As the narrative unfolds, we witness Job's steadfastness amidst overwhelming adversity. In a series of tragic events orchestrated by Satan with God's permission, Job loses his livestock, servants, and ultimately, his ten children—all in rapid succession. Yet, in the depths of his grief, Job responds with astonishing faith: "Naked I came from my mother's womb, and naked I will depart. The Lord gave and the Lord has taken away; may the name of the Lord be praised" (Job 1:21). These words reveal Job's profound trust in God's sovereignty, even when confronted with incomprehensible loss.

In the aftermath of these calamities, Job's suffering intensifies as he is afflicted with painful boils from head to toe. Despite his wife's urging to curse God and die, Job remains resolute. His friends, initially arriving to comfort him, soon engage in philosophical debates about the nature of suffering and God's justice. They argue that Job must have sinned to deserve such punishment, but Job vehemently defends his innocence, refusing to accept their simplistic explanations.

Throughout his ordeal, Job wrestles not only with physical agony but also with profound spiritual questions. He laments his condition, questioning why he was born only to endure such torment. Yet, amid his anguish, Job clings to his faith, declaring, "Though he slay me, yet will I hope in him" (Job 13:15). These words encapsulate Job's unwavering trust in God's wisdom and goodness, even in the midst of inexplicable suffering.

In the latter part of the book, God Himself addresses Job out of the whirlwind, revealing His divine wisdom and power. God's response challenges Job's limited understanding of His ways, emphasizing His sovereignty over all creation. Through this encounter, Job gains a deeper perspective on God's majestic nature and the complexity of His divine purposes.

Ultimately, after enduring this profound trial of faith, Job is restored twofold by God. His wealth is replenished, and he is blessed with new children. This restoration not only highlights God's faithfulness to those who trust Him but also underscores the resilience and enduring faith of Job throughout his arduous journey.

Job's story continues to resonate across centuries, offering profound insights into the nature of suffering, the sovereignty of God, and the transformative power of unwavering faith. It stands as a testament to the enduring truth that, even in our darkest moments, God remains faithful and His purposes prevail. Job's unwavering faith serves as a beacon of hope for believers facing trials, reminding us that through steadfast trust in God, we can find strength to endure and emerge victorious.

Job's narrative also challenges us to reconsider our perspectives on suffering and God's sovereignty. It prompts reflection on how we respond to adversity and our understanding of God's purposes in our lives. Through Job's example, we learn that faith is not immune to testing but is refined and strengthened in the crucible of suffering.

In conclusion, Job's journey exemplifies the profound depths of human suffering and the heights of spiritual resilience and trust in God. His story encourages us to persevere in faith, even when faced with overwhelming trials, and to trust in God's sovereign plan, knowing that His wisdom surpasses our understanding. Job's enduring faith serves as an enduring testimony to God's faithfulness and the transformative power of unwavering trust in Him.

Reflection and Application: Enduring Faith

Reflect on Job's Enduring Faith

1. **Understanding Job's Integrity:**

    a. **Question:** What qualities of Job's character made him stand out as a righteous man before God?

    b. **Reflection:** Consider how Job's integrity influenced his responses to adversity. His righteousness wasn't merely external but stemmed from a deep reverence and fear of God. Job's commitment to shunning evil and upholding justice set him apart as a man of unwavering faith.

    c. **Journal Prompt:** Write about a time in your life when you faced challenges to your faith. How did you respond? How did these challenges shape your understanding of God's faithfulness?

    d. **Additional Questions:** How did Job's integrity affect his relationships with his family and community? How can you cultivate integrity in your own life amidst adversity? What biblical principles can guide you in maintaining integrity in challenging situations?

2. **Trusting God in Adversity:**

    a. **Question:** How did Job's initial response to losing his possessions and children demonstrate his trust in God's sovereignty?

    b. **Reflection:** Job's immediate reaction, praising God even in the face of devastating loss, reflects his profound trust in God's sovereignty and goodness. His declaration, "The Lord gave and the Lord has taken away; may the name of the Lord be praised" (Job 1:21), underscores his unwavering faith amidst adversity.

    c. **Journal Prompt:** Describe a time when you had to trust God's plan despite not understanding the reasons behind your circumstances. What did you learn about God's character through that experience?

    d. **Additional Questions:** How can Job's response to adversity inspire you to trust God more deeply in your own trials? What practical steps can you take to cultivate a mindset of trust in God's sovereignty daily? How does trusting in God's sovereignty impact your decision-making in difficult situations?

3. **God's Sovereignty and Wisdom:**
4. a. **Question:** What did Job learn about God's sovereignty and wisdom through his encounter with God in the whirlwind?

    b. **Reflection:** Job's encounter with God in chapters 38-41 reveals God's majestic power and wisdom, far beyond human comprehension. Job learns that God's purposes are vast and intricately woven into the fabric of creation, challenging Job's limited understanding of divine justice.

    c. **Journal Prompt:** Reflect on a time when you struggled to understand why God allowed certain events in your life. How did your understanding of God's sovereignty help you trust Him more deeply?

    d. **Additional Questions:** How does God's sovereignty impact your view of suffering and adversity? In what ways can you align your life more closely with God's sovereign will? How can understanding God's sovereignty empower you to navigate uncertainty and challenges with faith and confidence?

5. **Endurance and Restoration:**

    a. **Question:** How did Job's endurance through suffering lead to his eventual restoration by God?

    b. **Reflection:** Job's endurance through unimaginable suffering and his unwavering faith in God's justice eventually lead to his restoration. God blesses Job twofold, restoring his wealth and granting him new children, illustrating God's faithfulness to those who remain steadfast in their faith.

    c. **Journal Prompt:** Describe a season in your life when you felt spiritually restored after enduring hardship. How did God's faithfulness during that time impact your faith journey?

    d. **Additional Questions:** How can Job's example of endurance inspire you to persevere through difficult seasons in your life? What role does forgiveness play in Job's restoration, and how can you apply this in your own life? How can God's promise of restoration encourage you to trust His timing in your current challenges?

Your Faith Journey

1. **Current Challenges:**

    a. **Question:** What are some current challenges in your life where you need to exercise faith, similar to Job?

    b. **Reflection:** Identify specific areas where you struggle to trust God completely amidst adversity. Job's story challenges us to trust God not only in prosperity but also in adversity, acknowledging His sovereignty over every aspect of our lives.

    c. **Journal Prompt:** Write about one or two situations you are currently facing where you need to exercise faith. What fears or doubts do you have? How can you remind yourself of God's promises and past faithfulness in these situations?

    d. **Additional Questions:** How can you distinguish between waiting on God's timing and taking action in response to challenges? What steps can you take to deepen your dependence on God in your current challenges? How can seeking wise counsel from fellow believers strengthen your faith journey through adversity?

2. **Role of Prayer and Scripture:**

    a. **Question:** How can prayer and studying God's Word strengthen your faith in the midst of challenges?

    b. **Reflection:** Prayer and scripture are essential tools in maintaining a vibrant faith. They provide spiritual nourishment, guidance, and strength, helping us to remain grounded in God's truth and promises during trials.

    c. **Journal Prompt:** Commit to a plan for prayer and Bible study that will help you grow in faith. Write out a prayer asking God for the strength and courage to trust Him more fully in the specific challenges you are currently facing.

    d. **Additional Questions:** How can consistent prayer deepen your relationship with God during times of adversity? In what ways does studying scripture provide practical wisdom and encouragement for navigating challenges? How can you integrate prayer and scripture into your daily routine to maintain spiritual resilience and trust in God's plan?

This workbook aims to guide you in reflecting deeply on Job's enduring faith, applying its lessons to your own life, and developing spiritual resilience amidst adversity. Use these questions and prompts to journal your thoughts, seek God's guidance, and grow in faith as you journey through challenges, trusting in God's sovereign plan.

Chapter 2: Hearing God's Voice

In our fast-paced, modern world, the multitude of distractions can make it difficult to hear and discern God's voice. From the constant buzz of technology to the demands of work and family, these distractions can cloud our spiritual hearing. John 10:27 provides reassurance, stating, "My sheep listen to my voice; I know them, and they follow me." This verse reminds us that, despite the chaos, we are capable of recognizing God's voice if we intentionally listen. However, this requires a conscious effort to quiet the external noise and focus on our relationship with God.

One major challenge in hearing God's voice is the overwhelming influence of other people's opinions. Social media, news outlets, and even well-meaning friends and family can offer conflicting advice and perspectives. In such times, it's essential to anchor ourselves in God's word. Proverbs 3:5-6 advises, "Trust in the Lord with all your heart and lean not on your own understanding; in all your ways submit to him, and he will make your paths straight." By prioritizing God's guidance over human opinions, we can better discern His voice and direction for our lives.

Work pressures and family problems can also hinder our ability to hear God. The demands of daily life often leave little room for quiet reflection and prayer. Yet, it's in these quiet moments that we are most likely to hear God's voice. Psalm 46:10 encourages us, "Be still, and know that I am God." Taking time to be still, to pray, and to meditate on God's word allows us to tune out the noise and focus on His presence. Regularly setting aside dedicated time for spiritual practices helps us develop a keener sense of His guidance amidst life's distractions.

Another obstacle to discerning God's voice is our own inner turmoil and doubts. Personal struggles and fears can create a cacophony within us, making it hard to recognize God's still, small voice. Isaiah 30:21 offers comfort, stating, "Whether you turn to the right or to the left, your ears will hear a voice behind you, saying, 'This is the way; walk in it.'" This verse reassures us that God's guidance is always available, even when we feel lost or overwhelmed. By fostering a deep, personal relationship with Him, we can learn to trust His voice above our internal doubts.

In conclusion, discerning God's voice in a world filled with noise and distractions requires intentional effort and spiritual discipline. By prioritizing God's word, setting aside time for quiet reflection, and trusting in His guidance, we can navigate through the chaos and clearly hear His voice. As believers, it's crucial to develop these practices to maintain a strong connection with God and follow His lead in every aspect of our lives.

Challenges in Discerning God's Voice

1. People's Opinions

People's opinions and advice can sometimes drown out God's voice, making it difficult to discern His will. Friends, family, and colleagues often have well-meaning intentions, but their perspectives may not always align with God's plan for us.

Scripture Reference: Proverbs 29:25 says, "Fear of man will prove to be a snare, but whoever trusts in the Lord is kept safe." This verse reminds us that while others' opinions can be influential, trusting in God should always be our priority.

2. Family Problems

Family issues can create emotional turmoil and stress, making it hard to focus on God's voice. When we are preoccupied with resolving conflicts or dealing with personal struggles within the family, our ability to seek and hear God's guidance can be compromised.

Scripture Reference: Matthew 10:37-39 states, "Anyone who loves their father or mother more than me is not worthy of me; anyone who loves their son or daughter more than me is not worthy of me. Whoever does not take up their cross and follow me is not worthy of me. Whoever finds their life will lose it, and whoever loses their life for my sake will find it." Jesus emphasizes the importance of prioritizing our relationship with Him above all else, even above family.

3. Work Pressures

Work-related stress and responsibilities can be overwhelming, leaving little room for quiet reflection and prayer. The constant demands of a busy schedule can crowd out time that could be spent in communion with God.

Scripture Reference: Matthew 6:33 encourages us, "But seek first his kingdom and his righteousness, and all these things will be given to you as well." This verse reminds us to prioritize our spiritual life, trusting that God will take care of our needs.

4. Noise and Distractions

The modern world is filled with constant noise and distractions from social media, news, entertainment, and technology. These distractions can keep us from spending quality time in God's presence, making it hard to hear His still, small voice.

Scripture Reference: Psalm 46:10 advises, "Be still, and know that I am God; I will be exalted among the nations, I will be exalted in the earth." This verse calls us to find moments of stillness where we can focus on God and listen for His voice.

Practical Steps to Discern God's Voice

1. **Regular Prayer and Meditation**: Establish a routine for prayer and meditation to quiet your mind and focus on God.

   Scripture Reference: Philippians 4:6-7 says, "Do not be anxious about anything, but in every situation, by prayer and petition, with thanksgiving, present your requests to God. And the peace of God, which transcends all understanding, will guard your hearts and your minds in Christ Jesus."

2. **Study the Bible**: Regularly reading and studying scripture helps you become familiar with God's character and His ways, making it easier to recognize His voice.

   Scripture Reference: Psalm 119:105 declares, "Your word is a lamp for my feet, a light on my path."

3. **Seek Godly Counsel**: Surround yourself with mature believers who can provide wise and godly advice, helping you discern God's voice amidst the noise.

   Scripture Reference: Proverbs 11:14 notes, "For lack of guidance a nation falls, but victory is won through many advisers."

4. **Create a Distraction-Free Environment**: Set aside specific times and places where you can be free from distractions to pray, meditate, and listen to God.

   Scripture Reference: Mark 1:35 describes Jesus' example, "Very early in the morning, while it was still dark, Jesus got up, left the house and went off to a solitary place, where he prayed."

By understanding these challenges and taking practical steps to address them, you can improve your ability to discern God's voice and follow His guidance more effectively.

Reflection and Application: Overcoming Challenges in Discerning God's Voice

This section is designed to help you process what you have read about the challenges in discerning God's voice and apply the lessons to your own life. Use this workbook to reflect deeply, journal your thoughts, and identify areas where you need to overcome obstacles to hear God's guidance more clearly.

Reflect on People's Opinions

1. **Influence of Others**:
    a. **Question**: How have other people's opinions influenced your decisions in the past?
    b. **Reflection**: Think about a time when you followed someone else's advice instead of seeking God's guidance. What was the outcome?
    c. **Journal Prompt**: Write about a situation where you felt torn between others' opinions and what you believed God was telling you. How did you navigate this conflict, and what did you learn from the experience?

Reflect on Family Problems

1. **Impact of Family Issues**:
    a. **Question**: In what ways have family problems distracted you from focusing on God's voice?
    b. **Reflection**: Consider a time when family issues were overwhelming. How did this affect your spiritual life and your ability to hear from God?
    c. **Journal Prompt**: Describe a family situation that has been particularly challenging for you. How can you seek God's guidance and maintain your focus on Him despite these challenges?

Reflect on Work Pressures

1. **Work-Related Stress**:
    a. **Question**: How does your job impact your ability to spend time with God and hear His voice?
    b. **Reflection**: Recall a period when work pressures consumed most of your time and energy. How did this affect your spiritual well-being?

Journal Prompt: Write about a time when work pressures made it difficult for you to connect with God. What steps can you take to create a better balance and prioritize your spiritual life

Reflect on Noise and Distractions

1. **Managing Distractions**:
    a. **Question**: What are the main distractions in your life that keep you from hearing God's voice?
    b. **Reflection**: Identify specific sources of noise and distraction in your daily routine. How do they affect your relationship with God?
    c. **Journal Prompt**: List the distractions that most commonly interfere with your time with God. What practical steps can you take to minimize these distractions and create a quiet space for prayer and reflection?

Your Personal Faith Journey

1. **Current Challenges**:
    a. **Question**: What are some current challenges in your life where you need to overcome obstacles to discern God's voice?
    b. **Reflection**: Think about areas where you struggle to hear from God due to various distractions and pressures.
    c. **Journal Prompt**: Write about one or two situations you are currently facing where you need to overcome challenges to discern God's voice. What specific steps can you take to address these challenges and focus more on God's guidance?

2. **Action Plan for Spiritual Growth**:
    a. **Question**: How can you develop a consistent practice of prayer, Bible study, and stillness to better hear God's voice?
    b. **Reflection**: Consider the role of spiritual disciplines in your life. How can you incorporate these practices more regularly?
    c. **Journal Prompt**: Create an action plan for developing a consistent routine of prayer, Bible study, and quiet time with God. Write out specific goals and steps you will take to cultivate a deeper, more attentive relationship with God.

Use these reflections, questions, and journal prompts as tools to deepen your faith and improve your ability to discern God's voice amidst life's challenges. Remember, discerning God's voice is a continual journey, and each step you take in trust and obedience brings you closer to His heart and His plans for your life.

We will share personal testimonies of individuals who have experienced God's guidance and the transformative power of obeying His voice. Isaiah 30:21 provides assurance: "Whether you turn to the right or to the left, your ears will hear a voice behind you, saying, 'This is the way; walk in it.

Personal Testimonies of Individuals Who Experienced God's Guidance and Transformative Power

Throughout the Bible, there are numerous individuals who have experienced God's guidance and the transformative power of obeying His voice. Here, we will discuss a few of these figures, exploring their personal testimonies and the impact of their obedience to God.

1. Joseph: From Prisoner to Prime Minister

Testimony: Joseph's life is a profound example of experiencing God's guidance and transformation. Sold into slavery by his brothers, Joseph faced numerous trials, including false accusations and imprisonment. Despite these hardships, Joseph remained faithful to God, interpreting dreams and trusting in God's plan.

Transformative Power: Joseph's obedience and trust in God led to his rise to power in Egypt, where he became second in command to Pharaoh. His position allowed him to save his family and many others from famine.

Scripture Reference: Genesis 50:20 captures Joseph's perspective, "You intended to harm me, but God intended it for good to accomplish what is now being done, the saving of many lives."

2. Esther: Courageous Queen

Testimony: Esther, a Jewish woman, became queen of Persia and found herself in a position to save her people from annihilation. When her uncle Mordecai urged her to speak to the king, she faced the potential penalty of death for approaching the king unsummoned.

Transformative Power: Esther's courageous obedience and willingness to risk her life led to the deliverance of the Jewish people. Her actions demonstrated the power of faith and the importance of standing up for what is right, even at great personal risk.

Scripture Reference: Esther 4:14 highlights her moment of decision, "For if you remain silent at this time, relief and deliverance for the Jews will arise from another place, but you and your father's family will perish. And who knows but that you have come to your royal position for such a time as this?"

3. Paul: From Persecutor to Apostle

Testimony: Paul, formerly known as Saul, was a fierce persecutor of Christians. On the road to Damascus, he encountered Jesus in a vision that transformed his life. Blinded and then healed, Paul was filled with the Holy Spirit and began preaching the gospel.

Transformative Power: Paul's obedience to God's calling led to the spread of Christianity throughout the Roman Empire. His letters, which form a significant part of the New Testament, continue to influence and inspire Christians today.

Scripture Reference: Acts 9:15-16 reveals God's plan for Paul, "But the Lord said to Ananias, 'Go! This man is my chosen instrument to proclaim my name to the Gentiles and their kings and to the people of Israel. I will show him how much he must suffer for my name.'"

4. Ruth: Loyalty and Faith

Testimony: Ruth, a Moabite widow, chose to remain with her Israelite mother-in-law Naomi, demonstrating remarkable loyalty and faith. Despite the uncertainty of their future, Ruth's dedication to Naomi and to the God of Israel never wavered.

Transformative Power: Ruth's obedience and faithfulness were rewarded when she married Boaz, a kinsman-redeemer, securing her and Naomi's future. Ruth's inclusion in the genealogy of Jesus (Matthew 1:5) highlights her significance in God's redemptive plan.

Scripture Reference: Ruth 1:16 shows her commitment, "But Ruth replied, 'Don't urge me to leave you or to turn back from you. Where you go I will go, and where you stay I will stay. Your people will be my people and your God my God.'"

5. Mary: The Mother of Jesus

Testimony: Mary, a young virgin, received a visit from the angel Gabriel, who announced that she would conceive and bear the Son of God. Despite the social stigma and personal challenges this would bring, Mary accepted God's will with humility and faith.

Transformative Power: Mary's obedience and willingness to serve God resulted in the birth of Jesus, the Savior of the world. Her faithfulness continues to be a model of submission to God's plan.

Scripture Reference: Luke 1:38 captures her response, "I am the Lord's servant," Mary answered. "May your word to me be fulfilled." Then the angel left her.

Reflection and Application: Personal Testimonies Workbook

Use this workbook section to reflect on the personal testimonies of these biblical figures and apply the lessons to your own life.

Reflect on Joseph's Testimony

1. **Facing Trials**:

    a. **Question**: How did Joseph's faith and obedience transform his situation?

    b. **Reflection**: Think about a challenging situation where you trusted God. What was the outcome?

c. **Journal Prompt**: Write about a time when you faced significant trials but saw God's hand at work. How did your faith help you through, and what did you learn from the experience?

Reflect on Esther's Testimony

1. **Courage and Faith**:

    a. **Question**: What can you learn from Esther's courage in facing potential danger?

    b. **Reflection**: Reflect on a moment when you had to make a difficult decision that required courage. How did your faith influence your choice

    c. **Journal Prompt**: Describe a situation where you needed to stand up for what was right, even at personal risk. How did you rely on your faith to guide you?

Reflect on Paul's Testimony

1. **Transformation and Calling**:

    a. **Question**: How did Paul's encounter with Jesus change his life and mission?

    b. **Reflection**: Consider how an encounter with God has transformed your life or calling.

    c. **Journal Prompt**: Write about a transformative experience in your spiritual journey. How did this encounter change your direction, and how have you followed God's calling since then

Reflect on Ruth's Testimony

1. **Loyalty and Trust**:

    a. **Question**: What does Ruth's story teach about loyalty and trust in God?

    b. **Reflection**: Think about a time when loyalty and trust in God led to unexpected blessings in your life.

    c. **Journal Prompt**: Reflect on a situation where you chose to remain faithful to God and others despite uncertainty. How did this decision impact your life?

Reflect on Mary's Testimony

1. **Submission to God's Will**:

    a. **Question**: How did Mary's acceptance of God's will demonstrate her faith?

    b. **Reflection**: Reflect on a time when you felt called to accept God's will, even when it was difficult.

    c. **Journal Prompt**: Describe a moment when you said "yes" to God's plan, despite personal challenges or fears. How did this decision affect your faith and life journey?

Use these reflections, questions, and journal prompts to deepen your understanding of God's guidance and the transformative power of obedience. Let the testimonies of these biblical figures inspire you to trust and follow God's voice in your own life.

Practical steps to cultivate a listening heart will be provided, helping you to develop a deeper, more intimate relationship with God, where His voice becomes clear and unmistakable. Revelation 3:20 highlights the importance of hearing God's voice: "Here I am! I stand at the door and knock. If anyone hears my voice and opens the door, I will come in and eat with that person, and they with me."

Cultivating a Listening Heart: Practical Steps for a Deeper Relationship with God

Developing a listening heart is essential for discerning God's voice and growing in intimacy with Him. Below are practical steps to help you cultivate a heart that is attuned to God's guidance, supported by scripture.

1. Regular Prayer and Communication with God

Step: Establish a consistent prayer routine to communicate with God, not just to present your requests but to listen for His guidance.

Scripture Reference: Philippians 4:6-7 advises, "Do not be anxious about anything, but in every situation, by prayer and petition, with thanksgiving, present your requests to God. And the peace of God, which transcends all understanding, will guard your hearts and your minds in Christ Jesus."

Practical Tip: Set aside specific times each day for prayer. Start with gratitude, present your needs, and spend quiet moments listening for God's response.

2. Meditate on Scripture

Step: Immerse yourself in God's Word to understand His character and recognize His voice.

Scripture Reference: Psalm 1:2-3 describes the blessings of meditating on God's law, "But whose delight is in the law of the Lord, and who meditates on his law day and night. That person is like a tree planted by streams of water, which yields its fruit in season and whose leaf does not wither—whatever they do prospers."

Practical Tip: Choose a specific book of the Bible or a set of verses to meditate on daily. Reflect on how these scriptures apply to your life and listen for what God is saying to you through them.

3. Practice Stillness and Silence

Step: Create regular times of stillness and silence to hear God's still, small voice amidst the noise of daily life.

Scripture Reference: Psalm 46:10 reminds us, "Be still, and know that I am God; I will be exalted among the nations, I will be exalted in the earth."

Practical Tip: Find a quiet place where you can sit in silence, free from distractions. Start with a few minutes each day, gradually increasing the time as you become more comfortable with silence.

4. Seek Godly Counsel

Step: Surround yourself with mature Christians who can provide wise and godly advice, helping you discern God's voice.

Scripture Reference: Proverbs 11:14 highlights the value of counsel, "For lack of guidance a nation falls, but victory is won through many advisers."

Practical Tip: Join a small group or find a spiritual mentor who can pray with you, offer guidance, and hold you accountable in your spiritual journey.

5. Cultivate an Obedient Heart

Step: Be willing to act on what you hear from God, demonstrating your trust and obedience.

Scripture Reference: James 1:22 encourages us to be doers of the word, "Do not merely listen to the word, and so deceive yourselves. Do what it says."

Practical Tip: Keep a journal of the impressions, scriptures, and messages you believe are from God. Reflect on these and take steps to act on them, even if they require faith and courage.

6. Fast and Seek God's Presence

Step: Engage in fasting as a way to draw closer to God, seeking His presence and direction.

Scripture Reference: Matthew 6:17-18 speaks about fasting, "But when you fast, put oil on your head and wash your face, so that it will not be obvious to others that you are fasting, but only to your Father, who is unseen; and your Father, who sees what is done in secret, will reward you."

Practical Tip: Choose a type of fast that is appropriate for you, whether it be food, media, or another distraction. Use the time you would normally spend on these activities to pray and seek God's presence.

7. Maintain a Heart of Worship

Step: Regularly engage in worship to keep your focus on God and cultivate a heart of gratitude and reverence.

Scripture Reference: Psalm 100:2 encourages us to, "Worship the Lord with gladness; come before him with joyful songs."

Practical Tip: Include worship in your daily routine, whether through singing, listening to worship music, or reading psalms. Let worship be a time to express your love for God and listen for His voice.

8. Be Patient and Persistent

Step: Cultivate patience and persistence, understanding that hearing God's voice is a journey that requires time and dedication.

Scripture Reference: Galatians 6:9 advises, "Let us not become weary in doing good, for at the proper time we will reap a harvest if we do not give up."

Practical Tip: Commit to these practices with the understanding that it may take time to develop a listening heart. Trust that God is with you in the process and that persistence will bear fruit.

By incorporating these practical steps into your daily life, you can develop a deeper, more intimate relationship with God, where His voice becomes clear and unmistakable. Remember, cultivating a listening heart is a continual journey that grows and deepens over time.

Chapter 3: Walking by Faith, Not by Sight

Walking by faith requires us to trust in the unseen and move forward based on God's promises rather than our own understanding. This concept is powerfully encapsulated in 2 Corinthians 5:7, which states, "For we live by faith, not by sight." This verse highlights the essence of faith—believing in what we cannot see and trusting in God's plans, even when they are not immediately visible. Faith calls us to rely on God's word and His promises, rather than our limited human perspective. It challenges us to step out of our comfort zones and trust that God is guiding our steps, even when the path is unclear.

The distinction between faith and sight is further elucidated in Hebrews 11:6, which teaches, "And without faith, it is impossible to please God, because anyone who comes to him must believe that he exists and that he rewards those who earnestly seek him." This verse underscores the fundamental nature of faith in our relationship with God. Faith is not merely a passive belief but an active pursuit of God's presence and promises. It involves earnestly seeking Him and trusting that He will reward our diligence and devotion. This kind of faith pleases God because it reflects a deep trust in His character and His word.

However, walking by faith often brings common doubts and fears. We may worry about the unknown, feel inadequate, or fear failure. These doubts can hinder our willingness to step out in faith. Proverbs 3:5-6 provides a powerful antidote to these fears: "Trust in the Lord with all your heart and lean not on your own understanding; in all your ways submit to him, and he will make your paths straight." This passage encourages us to fully trust in God, even when our understanding falls short. By submitting to Him and acknowledging His sovereignty, we can find the courage to overcome our fears and doubts, knowing that He will direct our paths.

One strategy to overcome doubts and fears is to immerse ourselves in God's word. Romans 10:17 states, "Consequently, faith comes from hearing the message, and the message is heard through the word about Christ." Regularly reading and meditating on Scripture strengthens our faith and reminds us of God's promises. Additionally, prayer is a vital practice for fortifying our faith. Philippians 4:6-7 encourages us, "Do not be anxious about anything, but in every situation, by prayer and petition, with thanksgiving, present your requests to God. And the peace of God, which transcends all understanding, will guard your hearts and your minds in Christ Jesus." By bringing our concerns to God in prayer, we can experience His peace and assurance.

Another effective approach is to reflect on past instances where God has been faithful. Remembering His past faithfulness can bolster our confidence in His future promises. Psalm 77:11-12 illustrates this practice: "I will remember the deeds of the Lord; yes, I will remember your miracles of long ago. I will consider all your works and meditate on all your mighty deeds." Reflecting on God's past interventions helps us trust that He will continue to guide and support us.

In conclusion, walking by faith involves trusting in God's promises and moving forward despite our doubts and fears. By relying on Scripture, engaging in prayer, and remembering God's past faithfulness, we can cultivate a robust faith that pleases God and guides us through life's uncertainties. As believers, it's essential to develop these strategies to maintain a strong, unwavering faith in God's unchanging character and promises.

Faith vs. Sight and the Importance of Relying on God's Word

In our journey as believers, understanding the distinction between faith and sight is paramount. Faith, as defined in Hebrews 11:1, is the assurance of things hoped for, the conviction of things not seen. This biblical faith calls us to trust in God and His promises even when our physical senses or current circumstances offer no tangible evidence. In contrast, living by sight involves relying on our human understanding, experiences, and the visible world around us. This approach can often lead to uncertainty, fear, and discouragement, as our perception is inherently limited and fallible.

Living by sight confines us to what we can see and comprehend, making us prone to doubt and anxiety. We may find ourselves questioning God's plans and purposes when faced with trials and challenges. However, Proverbs 3:5-6 provides a divine remedy: "Trust in the Lord with all your heart and lean not on your own understanding; in all your ways acknowledge him, and he will make your paths straight." This scripture encourages us to shift our reliance from our own understanding to God's infinite wisdom and guidance.

Conversely, living by faith requires us to trust God's character and His Word, even when our circumstances seem contrary. Hebrews 11:6 underscores the essence of faith, stating, "And without faith it is impossible to please God, because anyone who comes to him must believe that he exists and that he rewards those who earnestly seek him." This verse highlights two crucial aspects of faith: belief in God's existence and confidence in His benevolence. True faith involves a deep, unwavering trust in God's goodness and His commitment to fulfill His promises.

God's Word serves as the foundation for our faith. It is through the scriptures that we learn about His nature, His promises, and His plans for us. Romans 10:17 states, "So then faith comes by hearing, and hearing by the word of God." Immersing ourselves in the Bible strengthens our faith, providing the spiritual nourishment needed to trust God wholeheartedly. The stories of biblical figures like Abraham, who believed God's promise of numerous descendants despite his and Sarah's old age, inspire us to live by faith. Abraham's unwavering trust in God, even when the promise seemed impossible, was credited to him as righteousness (Genesis 15:5-6).

Another profound example is Peter's experience of walking on water. As long as Peter kept his eyes on Jesus, he walked on the water by faith. However, when he shifted his focus to the stormy waves, he began to sink, illustrating the perils of living by sight (Matthew 14:28-31). These accounts remind us that faith is about maintaining our focus on God and His Word, regardless of the external circumstances.

In practical terms, cultivating a life of faith involves daily devotion to God's Word, consistent prayer, and seeking fellowship with other believers. These practices help us to anchor our trust in God, enabling us to navigate life's uncertainties with confidence and peace. By relying on God's promises and His faithfulness, we can experience the fullness of life that comes from living by faith and not by sight.

Overcoming Doubts and Fears When Stepping Out in Faith

When we decide to step out in faith, it is natural to experience doubts and fears. These feelings can stem from various sources: fear of failure, fear of the unknown, or even fear of not being adequate enough. However, the Bible offers profound wisdom and guidance to help us overcome these challenges. One of the foundational scriptures that addresses overcoming fear is Proverbs 3:5-6: "Trust in the Lord with all your heart and lean not on your own understanding; in all your ways submit to him, and he will make your paths straight." This verse encourages us to place our complete trust in God rather than relying solely on our understanding and abilities.

To build trust and overcome doubts, regularly spend time in prayer, seeking God's guidance and strength. Meditating on scriptures that reinforce God's promises and faithfulness, such as Philippians 4:6-7, reminds us to present our requests to God with thanksgiving, easing our anxieties. Affirming God's promises by writing down and frequently reciting Bible verses that speak against fear and doubt can be incredibly powerful. For instance, Isaiah 41:10 states, "So do not fear, for I am with you; do not be dismayed, for I am your God. I will strengthen you and help you; I will uphold you with my righteous right hand." Keeping a faith journal to document how God has previously answered prayers and guided you through difficult times can also reinforce your trust in Him.

Surrounding yourself with a community of believers who can provide support, encouragement, and godly wisdom is essential. Proverbs 15:22 says, "Plans fail for lack of counsel, but with many advisers they succeed." Joining a Bible study group or finding a mentor who can help you grow in your faith and provide perspective during challenging times can be invaluable. Additionally, breaking down your faith journey into smaller, manageable steps can make the process less overwhelming. Celebrate each step of obedience and progress, no matter how small it may seem. Reflecting on James 1:5-6, which advises asking God for wisdom and believing without doubting, can help you stay focused and confident.

Reminding yourself of God's faithfulness in the past is another powerful strategy. Just as David remembered God's help when facing Goliath (1 Samuel 17:37), recalling past victories can strengthen your confidence in God's provision and protection. Keeping a gratitude journal to note daily blessings and answered prayers reinforces the awareness of God's ongoing work in your life. To internalize these strategies, incorporate practical exercises into your daily routine. Spend a few minutes each day reflecting on a specific scripture and how it applies to your current situation. Use the workbook journal aspect of this e-book to write down your fears and doubts, and then write a corresponding scripture that counters each fear, turning your focus back to God's word. Finding a prayer partner with whom you can regularly share your journey, pray together, and hold each other accountable in faith can also provide immense support.

Walking by faith requires intentionality and perseverance. By trusting in the Lord, leaning on His understanding, and employing these strategies, you can overcome doubts and fears. Remember that faith is a journey, and each step taken in trust and obedience brings you closer to the fulfillment of God's promises in your life.

Chapter 4: Standing Firm in the Storm

Life's storms are inevitable, but our response to them determines our spiritual growth. James 1:2-4 encourages us to "Consider it pure joy, my brothers and sisters, whenever you face trials of many kinds, because you know that the testing of your faith produces perseverance. Let perseverance finish its work so that you may be mature and complete, not lacking anything." This passage underscores the transformative power of trials. Rather than viewing challenges as setbacks, we are called to see them as opportunities for growth. The testing of our faith through life's storms develops perseverance, which in turn leads to spiritual maturity and completeness.

Recognizing and confronting the storms we face is crucial for our spiritual journey. Psalm 46:1-3 reassures us, "God is our refuge and strength, an ever-present help in trouble. Therefore we will not fear, though the earth give way and the mountains fall into the heart of the sea, though its waters roar and foam and the mountains quake with their surging." This scripture provides a powerful reminder of God's constant presence and support. No matter how tumultuous our circumstances, we can find refuge and strength in God. By focusing on His steadfastness, we can confront our challenges with confidence, knowing that He is our unwavering anchor.

To remain steadfast in faith during difficult times, we need practical strategies. One effective approach is to immerse ourselves in God's word, finding comfort and guidance in scripture. Philippians 4:6-7 advises, "Do not be anxious about anything, but in every situation, by prayer and petition, with thanksgiving, present your requests to God. And the peace of God, which transcends all understanding, will guard your hearts and your minds in Christ Jesus." By turning to prayer and thanksgiving, we can shift our focus from our troubles to God's faithfulness, allowing His peace to guard our hearts and minds.

Sharing encouraging stories of individuals who have triumphed over adversity through unwavering faith can also inspire and uplift us. These testimonies serve as tangible reminders that God is faithful and powerful, even in the most turbulent situations. For instance, the story of Job demonstrates incredible perseverance and trust in God despite immense suffering. Job 1:21 reflects his unwavering faith: "The Lord gave and the Lord has taken away; may the name of the Lord be praised." Job's story encourages us to hold on to our faith, trusting that God has a greater purpose even in our pain.

Another comforting promise is found in Isaiah 43:2: "When you pass through the waters, I will be with you; and when you pass through the rivers, they will not sweep over you. When you walk through the fire, you will not be burned; the flames will not set you ablaze." This verse reassures us of God's presence and protection in the midst of our trials. No matter what we face, God is with us, guiding us through the challenges and ensuring that we are not overcome by them.

In conclusion, life's storms are opportunities for spiritual growth, shaping us into mature and complete believers. By relying on God's word, engaging in prayer, and drawing inspiration from stories of faith, we can remain steadfast in our faith during difficult times. Trusting in God's constant presence and His promises, we can face our challenges with courage and confidence, knowing that He is with us every step of the way.

I Told the Storm

The story of Shadrach, Meshach, and Abednego is a powerful testament to standing firm in the storm, demonstrating unwavering faith in the face of extreme adversity. These three young men, along with Daniel, were taken captive from Judah and brought to Babylon. In Daniel 3, King Nebuchadnezzar erected a massive golden statue and commanded everyone to bow down and worship it, threatening death in a fiery furnace for anyone who refused. Shadrach, Meshach, and Abednego, steadfast in their faith in the one true God, refused to bow down to the idol. Their bold response to the king was a profound declaration of trust in God's sovereignty: "If we are thrown into the blazing furnace, the God we serve is able to deliver us from it... But even if he does not, we want you to know, Your Majesty, that we will not serve your gods or worship the image of gold you have set up" (Daniel 3:17-18).

Despite the king's fury and the furnace being heated seven times hotter than usual, the three men remained resolute. They were bound and thrown into the furnace, but to everyone's astonishment, they walked unharmed in the fire, accompanied by a fourth figure who appeared to be a divine presence. King Nebuchadnezzar, witnessing this miracle, called them out, and they emerged unscathed, without even the smell of fire on their clothes. This miraculous deliverance not only demonstrated God's power to save but also inspired the king to praise the God of Shadrach, Meshach, and Abednego, acknowledging His supreme authority.

Their story encourages believers to stand firm in their faith, regardless of the consequences, and trust that God is with them in every trial. It serves as a reminder that God honors and protects those who remain faithful to Him, even in the most dangerous and seemingly hopeless situations. This is echoed in Isaiah 43:2, where God promises, "When you pass through the waters, I will be with you; and when you pass through the rivers, they will not sweep over you. When you walk through the fire, you will not be burned; the flames will not set you ablaze." Additionally, 1 Peter 1:6-7 reassures us that our trials refine our faith: "In all this you greatly rejoice, though now for a little while you may have had to suffer grief in all kinds of trials. These have come so that the proven genuineness of your faith—of greater worth than gold, which perishes even though refined by fire—may result in praise, glory and honor when Jesus Christ is revealed."

The steadfast faith of Shadrach, Meshach, and Abednego exemplifies how we can stand firm in the storm, knowing that God is present with us and will use our trials to strengthen and purify our faith.

Consider the story of Hagar, an Egyptian slave who faced abandonment in the wilderness with her son Ishmael. Hagar's journey began with being mistreated and cast out by Sarah, Abraham's wife. Alone and desperate, Hagar cried out to God, who heard her distress and provided a miraculous well of water to sustain them. This story from Genesis 21:8-21 demonstrates God's compassion and faithfulness, even in the most dire circumstances. Hagar's unwavering trust in God's provision, despite her marginalized status, serves as a powerful example of how God sees and cares for those who are overlooked or oppressed. Her story encourages us to trust in God's presence and provision, even when life's challenges seem insurmountable, knowing that He is with us through every trial and will make a way where there seems to be none.

In life, we are promised storms—challenges, trials, and tribulations that test our faith and perseverance. These storms can take various forms: personal struggles, loss, uncertainty, or even opposition for our beliefs. However, as Christians, our response to these storms is crucial, shaping our spiritual growth and resilience. The Bible offers profound wisdom on this matter. James 1:2-4 encourages us to "consider it pure joy, my brothers and sisters, whenever you face trials of many kinds, because you know that the testing of your faith produces perseverance. Let perseverance finish its work so that you may be mature and complete, not lacking anything." This passage underscores the transformative power of trials, suggesting that through them, our faith is refined and strengthened. Similarly, in Matthew 8:23-27, Jesus calms a storm, demonstrating his authority over nature and teaching his disciples about trust amid turbulence. The disciples' fear and Jesus' calm response illustrate the contrast between worldly anxiety and steadfast faith. Through these biblical narratives, we learn that storms are opportunities for spiritual growth—challenges that, when faced with faith and reliance on God's promises, can deepen our understanding, strengthen our character, and ultimately bring us closer to God's purpose for our lives. Therefore, while life's storms are inevitable, our response guided by scripture can lead to profound spiritual maturation and a deeper connection with God.

Consider the unnamed widow of Zarephath, encountered by the prophet Elijah during a severe famine (1 Kings 17:8-16). This widow was preparing to eat her last meal with her son before they expected to die from starvation. Despite her dire circumstances, when Elijah asked her for food, she demonstrated remarkable faith by obeying his request. Miraculously, her flour and oil did not run out throughout the entire famine, sustaining her household until the drought ended. This unnamed widow's story illustrates the power of trusting in God's provision, even when resources are depleted, and hope seems lost.

Another unusual figure is the Roman centurion whose faith impressed Jesus (Matthew 8:5-13). As a Gentile military officer, he approached Jesus with a request to heal his paralyzed servant. The centurion expressed profound faith, declaring that Jesus only needed to speak the word for his servant to be healed. Jesus marveled at his faith, stating that he had not found such great faith even in Israel. This centurion's story challenges conventional expectations, showing that faith transcends cultural and religious boundaries, and that God honors sincere belief regardless of background or social status.

These stories of the unnamed widow and the Roman centurion highlight the diversity of God's work through individuals who exhibit extraordinary faith in unexpected circumstances. They encourage us to trust in God's power and provision, even in situations where conventional wisdom might suggest hopelessness or impossibility.

Reflection and Application: Standing Firm in the Storm

Shadrach, Meshach, and Abednego

Thought-Provoking Questions:

1. How would you react if faced with a situation where standing firm in your faith could result in severe consequences?

2. What can we learn from the faith of Shadrach, Meshach, and Abednego about trusting God in seemingly impossible situations?

3. How does their story inspire you to confront your own fears and challenges with faith?

Journal Prompts:

1. Reflect on a time when you had to make a difficult decision that tested your faith. How did you handle it, and what was the outcome?

2. Write about a current or past situation where you felt overwhelmed by the "fire" of life's challenges. How can you draw strength from the story of Shadrach, Meshach, and Abednego?

3. Pray and journal about an area in your life where you need to trust God more. Ask Him for the courage and faith to stand firm in that situation.

Hagar

Thought-Provoking Questions:

1. How does Hagar's story show that God sees and hears us, even when we feel abandoned or marginalized?

2. What aspects of Hagar's faith can you apply to your own life when you face feelings of isolation or despair?

3. How can Hagar's experience of God's provision in the wilderness inspire you to trust God's care in your own "desert" experiences?

Journal Prompts:

1. Write about a time when you felt unseen or unheard. How did you cope with those feelings, and where can you see God's hand in that situation now?

2. Reflect on how God provided for Hagar and Ishmael in the wilderness. What are some ways God has provided for you in difficult times?

3. Journal a prayer asking God to reveal His presence and provision in areas of your life where you feel alone or abandoned

The Widow of Zarephath

Thought-Provoking Questions:

1. How does the widow of Zarephath's willingness to give her last meal to Elijah demonstrate her faith in God's provision?

2. What can you learn from her story about generosity and trust in God, especially when resources are scarce?

3. How does her experience challenge you to trust God with your own resources and to step out in faith?

Journal Prompts:

1. Think of a time when you were called to give or act in faith, even when it seemed like you didn't have enough. What was the outcome, and how did it impact your faith?

2. Reflect on the concept of trusting God with your resources. How can you apply the widow's example to your life today?

3. Write a prayer of thanksgiving for the ways God has provided for you in the past and ask for the courage to trust Him with your future needs.

The Roman Centurion

Thought-Provoking Questions:

1. What stands out to you about the Roman centurion's faith in Jesus' authority, and how does it compare to your own faith?

2. How can you apply the centurion's example of humble yet confident faith to situations in your life where you need healing or intervention?

3. In what ways does the centurion's story encourage you to break down barriers of doubt or cultural expectations in your faith journey?

Journal Prompts:

1. Write about an area in your life where you need to trust Jesus' authority and power. How can you adopt the centurion's attitude of faith in this situation?

2. Reflect on any doubts or cultural expectations that may be hindering your faith. How can you overcome these barriers?

3. Journal a prayer asking Jesus for the same kind of confident faith the centurion had, trusting Him to work powerfully in your life.

Chapter 5: The Nehemiah Principle

Nehemiah's story is a powerful example of dedication and faithfulness. Nehemiah 6:3 illustrates his commitment: "So I sent messengers to them with this reply: 'I am carrying on a great project and cannot go down. Why should the work stop while I leave it and go down to you?'" This chapter takes a deep dive into his unwavering commitment to rebuilding Jerusalem's walls despite intense opposition. We will extract valuable lessons from Nehemiah's life, showing how his principles can be applied to our own lives. Nehemiah 4:14 shows his courage: "After I looked things over, I stood up and said to the nobles, the officials and the rest of the people, 'Don't be afraid of them. Remember the Lord, who is great and awesome, and fight for your families, your sons and your daughters, your wives and your homes.'" Readers will learn how to stay focused on their God-given tasks, avoiding distractions and standing firm in their purpose, just as Nehemiah did. Nehemiah 2:18 highlights the power of collective effort: "I also told them about the gracious hand of my God on me and what the king had said to me. They replied, 'Let us start rebuilding.' So they began this good work."

The Nehemiah Principle, derived from the story of Nehemiah in the Old Testament, teaches the importance of staying focused on one's mission and not allowing distractions to derail progress. Nehemiah was a cupbearer to the Persian king Artaxerxes, and upon hearing about the dilapidated state of Jerusalem's walls, he was deeply moved to take action. With the king's blessing, Nehemiah returned to Jerusalem to oversee the reconstruction of the city's walls, a monumental task that required immense dedication and perseverance.

Throughout the project, Nehemiah faced numerous distractions and opposition, primarily from neighboring enemies who sought to thwart his efforts. Sanballat, Tobiah, and Geshem, key antagonists in the narrative, repeatedly tried to lure Nehemiah away from his work through various tactics, including mockery, threats, and deceptive invitations to meet and discuss. Recognizing these ploys as distractions, Nehemiah consistently refused to be drawn away from his mission. His steadfast focus is encapsulated in his response to them: "I am carrying on a great project and cannot go down. Why should the work stop while I leave it and go down to you?" (Nehemiah 6:3).

Nehemiah's unwavering commitment to his task despite external pressures offers a powerful lesson for us today. In our own lives, distractions can come in many forms—people who do not understand or support our goals, social obligations, or even our own fears and doubts. Like Nehemiah, we must discern which activities and interactions genuinely contribute to our mission and which ones are merely distractions that can impede our progress. This principle encourages us to set clear boundaries, prioritize our tasks, and remain focused on our objectives, even when it means saying no to others.

Nehemiah's determination and clarity of purpose remind us that achieving significant goals often requires a singular focus and the ability to shut out distractions. By adhering to the Nehemiah Principle, we can ensure that our time and energy are devoted to what truly matters, allowing us to accomplish our goals with excellence and integrity. This disciplined approach not only helps in achieving personal and professional aspirations but also fosters a sense of fulfillment and purpose, knowing that we are dedicating our efforts to meaningful endeavors.

Reflection and Application: The Nehemiah Principle

Nehemiah's Mission

Thought-Provoking Questions:

1. How did Nehemiah's clear sense of purpose help him resist the distractions and opposition he faced?

2. What specific tactics did Nehemiah use to stay focused on rebuilding Jerusalem's walls despite external pressures?

3. How can you identify the "Sanballats" and "Tobiahs" in your own life—people or situations that attempt to distract you from your mission?

Journal Prompts:

1. Reflect on a time when you were deeply committed to a project or goal. What distractions did you face, and how did you handle them?

2. Write about a current goal or mission in your life. List potential distractions and how you plan to stay focused despite them.

3. Journal a prayer asking for the discernment and strength to stay dedicated to your goals, just as Nehemiah did, despite any opposition you might encounter.

Identifying Distractions

Thought-Provoking Questions:

1. What are common distractions in your daily life that pull you away from your most important tasks?

2. How do these distractions affect your progress and overall productivity?

3. What steps can you take to minimize or eliminate these distractions

Journal Prompts:

1. List the top three distractions you face regularly. Reflect on how they impact your work and personal goals.

2. Write about a specific instance where you successfully overcame a distraction. What strategies did you use, and what was the outcome?

3. Plan and journal about practical steps you can take to reduce distractions in your life. Consider setting boundaries, creating a focused work environment, or establishing a routine.

Setting Boundaries

Thought-Provoking Questions:

1. How did Nehemiah set boundaries to protect his work on the wall from being interrupted?

2. In what areas of your life do you need to establish stronger boundaries to stay focused on your goals?

3. How can setting boundaries enhance your productivity and help you achieve your objectives?

Journal Prompts:

1. Reflect on an area of your life where you feel overwhelmed by distractions or interruptions. How can setting boundaries help you manage this better?

2. Write about a time when setting a boundary improved your focus and productivity. What boundary did you set, and what was the result?

3. Journal a commitment to set one new boundary this week that will help you stay focused on an important goal. Describe the boundary and how you will implement it.

Maintaining Focus

Thought-Provoking Questions:

1. What can you learn from Nehemiah's determination and clarity of purpose about maintaining focus on long-term goals?

2. How do you currently stay focused on your tasks, and where could you improve?

3. What role does faith play in helping you stay committed to your mission, even when faced with distractions?

Journal Prompts:

1. Reflect on your current methods for maintaining focus. Are they effective? Why or why not?

2. Write about a goal you are passionate about. Describe the steps you will take to maintain your focus and ensure you achieve it.

3. Journal a prayer for strength and clarity, asking God to help you stay focused and committed to your mission, just as Nehemiah did.

Chapter 6: Overcoming Opposition

Opposition and distractions are inevitable when pursuing God's calling. Isaiah 54:17 assures us, "No weapon forged against you will prevail, and you will refute every tongue that accuses you. This is the heritage of the servants of the Lord, and this is their vindication from me, declares the Lord." This chapter will help you identify the sources of such challenges and provides practical advice on dealing with criticism and naysayers. By strengthening your resolve to follow God's instructions, you will be equipped to overcome any obstacles that come your way.

Romans 8:31 asks, "What, then, shall we say in response to these things? If God is for us, who can be against us?" This powerful question underscores the unwavering support believers have in God's divine protection and guidance. It encourages us to draw strength from our faith, knowing that God's favor outweighs any opposition we may face. Throughout history and in our lives today, countless examples demonstrate how individuals persevered through adversity by trusting in God's promises.

Drawing from real-life examples and biblical insights, this chapter emphasizes the importance of staying true to God's direction, regardless of external pressures. It illustrates how figures like Joseph, despite being sold into slavery and facing unjust accusations, remained faithful to God's plan, ultimately rising to prominence. Their stories remind us that God's purposes prevail over adversity when we steadfastly follow His will.

1 Peter 5:8-9 warns, "Be alert and of sober mind. Your enemy the devil prowls around like a roaring lion looking for someone to devour. Resist him, standing firm in the faith, because you know that the family of believers throughout the world is undergoing the same kind of sufferings." This passage highlights the spiritual battle believers face, where the adversary seeks to undermine faith and sow discord. By staying vigilant and grounded in faith, we can resist these attacks and remain steadfast in God's truth.

In navigating opposition and distractions, it's essential to recognize that challenges can strengthen our faith and deepen our reliance on God. The Apostle Paul, who endured persecution and hardships throughout his ministry, proclaimed in 2 Corinthians 4:8-9, "We are hard pressed on every side, but not crushed; perplexed, but not in despair; persecuted, but not abandoned; struck down, but not destroyed." His resilience underscores the transformative power of faith in overcoming adversity.

Therefore, as you embark on your journey of faith and obedience to God's calling, remember that His promises are steadfast. By embracing these truths and drawing strength from biblical wisdom and personal testimonies, you can navigate opposition with resilience and unwavering faith. Just as God sustained His servants throughout history, He remains faithful today, empowering you to overcome every obstacle and fulfill His purpose in your life.

Dealing with Opposition and Criticism

In life, opposition and criticism are inevitable, especially when pursuing significant goals or living out one's faith. The story of Nehemiah provides valuable insights into identifying sources of opposition and overcoming such challenges with faith and determination. Nehemiah faced several sources of opposition while rebuilding Jerusalem's walls. His primary adversaries were Sanballat, Tobiah, and Geshem, who used various tactics to discourage and distract him. They mocked and ridiculed the workers (Nehemiah 4:1-3), attempted to instill fear through threats (Nehemiah 4:7-8), and tried to deceive Nehemiah into leaving his work (Nehemiah 6:2). Despite these challenges, Nehemiah remained steadfast, responding with prayer, strategic planning, and unwavering focus on his mission.

To overcome such challenges, it's essential to stay rooted in God's Word and seek His guidance. Scriptures like Isaiah 41:10 remind us, "So do not fear, for I am with you; do not be dismayed, for I am your God. I will strengthen you and help you; I will uphold you with my righteous right hand." Additionally, James 1:2-4 encourages us to view trials as opportunities for growth: "Consider it pure joy, my brothers and sisters, whenever you face trials of many kinds, because you know that the testing of your faith produces perseverance. Let perseverance finish its work so that you may be mature and complete, not lacking anything." Practical advice for dealing with criticism and naysayers includes maintaining a clear sense of purpose, setting boundaries, and surrounding yourself with supportive individuals who share your vision. It's crucial to discern between constructive criticism, which can be beneficial, and negative criticism intended to discourage or distract. When faced with opposition, take a step back, pray for wisdom, and respond with grace and firmness, just as Nehemiah did.

One key aspect of overcoming opposition is maintaining a strong and consistent prayer life. Nehemiah frequently turned to prayer in times of trouble, seeking God's guidance and strength. Nehemiah 4:9 states, "But we prayed to our God and posted a guard day and night to meet this threat." This verse highlights the importance of combining prayer with practical action. By seeking God's direction and taking tangible steps to protect and advance his mission, Nehemiah set an example of balanced faith and action. For modern believers, cultivating a habit of regular prayer and seeking God's wisdom can provide clarity and strength when facing opposition. Remembering that God is our ultimate source of support can help us remain resolute and undeterred in our pursuits.

Another vital strategy is to keep focused on the mission and avoid distractions. Nehemiah's adversaries tried various schemes to lure him away from his work, but he remained undistracted. Nehemiah 6:3 captures his response: "So I sent messengers to them with this reply: 'I am carrying on a great project and cannot go down. Why should the work stop while I leave it and go down to you?'" This unwavering focus allowed Nehemiah to complete the wall despite relentless opposition. In our own lives, staying focused on God's calling requires setting clear priorities and refusing to be sidetracked by critics or distractions. Developing a clear vision and reminding ourselves of our goals can help maintain momentum and progress, even when facing resistance.

Lastly, it's important to build a supportive community. Nehemiah surrounded himself with like-minded individuals who shared his vision and were committed to the work. He appointed capable leaders and organized the workers effectively, fostering a sense of unity and purpose. This collaborative approach not only enhanced productivity but also provided encouragement and strength during difficult times. For us, engaging with a community of believers who share our values and goals can provide much-needed support and encouragement. Hebrews 10:24-25 advises, "And let us consider how we may spur one another on toward love and good deeds, not giving up meeting together, as some are in the habit of doing, but encouraging one another—and all the more as you see the Day approaching." By building a network of support, we can draw strength from each other and remain resilient in the face of opposition.

In conclusion, dealing with opposition and criticism requires a combination of prayer, focus, and community support. By following Nehemiah's example and relying on God's guidance, we can overcome challenges and remain steadfast in our mission. Opposition, though challenging, can serve as a catalyst for growth and deeper reliance on God. As we navigate criticism and resistance, let us remember that God is with us, providing strength and direction every step of the way.

Reflection and Application: Dealing with Opposition and Criticism

Identifying Sources of Opposition

Thought-Provoking Questions:

1. What types of opposition did Nehemiah face while rebuilding the walls of Jerusalem?
2. How did Nehemiah recognize and address these sources of opposition without being derailed from his mission?
3. What are some common sources of opposition you encounter in your own life?

Journal Prompts:

1. Reflect on a time when you faced significant opposition to a goal or project. Who or what was the source of this opposition?
2. Write about how you identified the opposition and how it impacted your progress.
3. Pray and journal about ways to recognize and address sources of opposition in your current endeavors.

Overcoming Challenges

Thought-Provoking Questions:

1. How did Nehemiah's faith and strategic planning help him overcome the challenges he faced?
2. What specific actions did Nehemiah take to ensure the completion of the wall despite continuous threats?
3. How can you apply Nehemiah's strategies to overcome challenges in your own life?

Journal Prompts:

1. Describe a challenging situation you are currently facing. What steps can you take to address and overcome this challenge?
2. Reflect on a past challenge that you successfully overcame. What strategies did you use, and what role did your faith play in the process?
3. Journal a prayer asking for God's guidance and strength to overcome your current challenges, drawing inspiration from Nehemiah's example.

Dealing with Criticism and Naysayers

Thought-Provoking Questions:

1. How did Nehemiah handle criticism and mockery from his adversaries?
2. What role did prayer and faith play in Nehemiah's response to criticism?
3. How can you differentiate between constructive criticism and negative, discouraging criticism?

Journal Prompts:

1. Think about a time when you received criticism. How did you react, and what was the outcome?
2. Write about how you can respond to criticism in a way that is constructive and aligns with your faith.
3. Reflect on Proverbs 15:31-32: "Whoever heeds life-giving correction will be at home among the wise. Those who disregard discipline despise themselves, but the one who heeds correction gains understanding." How can this scripture guide your response to criticism?

Practical Advice for Dealing with Opposition

Thought-Provoking Questions:

1. What practical steps did Nehemiah take to protect his work and his people from opposition?
2. How can setting boundaries help you stay focused and resilient in the face of opposition?
3. What role does a supportive community play in overcoming challenges and staying focused on your goals?

Journal Prompts:

1. Reflect on an area in your life where you need to set stronger boundaries to protect your goals. What specific actions can you take?
2. Write about the people who support and encourage you in your mission. How can you cultivate and strengthen these relationships?
3. Journal a commitment to seek out and nurture a supportive community that will help you stay focused and resilient in the face of opposition.

Chapter 7: The Power of God's Promises

God's promises are powerful and unwavering. Joshua 21:45 testifies, "Not one of all the Lord's good promises to Israel failed; everyone was fulfilled." This chapter helps you understand and claim these promises in your own life. Through real-life examples of God's faithfulness, we will illustrate how trusting in His promises can bring about miraculous outcomes. 2 Corinthians 1:20 confirms, "For no matter how many promises God has made, they are 'Yes' in Christ. And so, through him the 'Amen' is spoken by us to the glory of God." Encouragement to trust in God's timing and remain patient will be provided, assuring you that His promises are sure and will come to pass, no matter how long the wait. Hebrews 10:23 urges, "Let us hold unswervingly to the hope we profess, for he who promised is faithful."

To fully grasp the significance of God's promises, it's essential to delve into His Word and understand the context in which these promises were made. The Bible is replete with assurances from God, each demonstrating His unwavering commitment to His people. For example, the promise of peace in Philippians 4:7, "And the peace of God, which transcends all understanding, will guard your hearts and your minds in Christ Jesus," offers comfort in times of anxiety. Similarly, the promise of provision in Philippians 4:19, "And my God will meet all your needs according to the riches of his glory in Christ Jesus," reassures us that God is aware of and will provide for our needs. Reflecting on these promises and their fulfillment in the lives of biblical characters and contemporary believers strengthens our faith and trust in God's faithfulness.

One profound way to claim God's promises is through prayer and declaration of His Word. By praying scripture, we align our desires and needs with God's will, inviting His promises to manifest in our lives. For instance, if facing a challenging situation, declaring Jeremiah 29:11, "For I know the plans I have for you," declares the Lord, "plans to prosper you and not to harm you, plans to give you hope and a future," reinforces our confidence in God's sovereign plans. Additionally, maintaining a prayer journal to record prayers and God's subsequent answers can serve as a powerful testament to His faithfulness over time. This practice not only helps in recognizing God's active involvement in our lives but also provides encouragement during times of waiting and uncertainty.

Trusting in God's timing is another critical aspect of experiencing His promises. Often, there is a waiting period between the promise and its fulfillment, which can test our faith and patience. However, understanding that God's timing is perfect and far beyond our comprehension can bring immense peace. Ecclesiastes 3:11 reminds us, "He has made everything beautiful in its time." This perspective helps us embrace the process, knowing that God's delays are not denials but are part of His perfect plan for our growth and preparation. Reflecting on the stories of Abraham and Sarah, Joseph, and others who experienced long periods of waiting before seeing God's promises fulfilled can inspire us to remain steadfast and hopeful.

Moreover, real-life testimonies of individuals who have experienced God's faithfulness can be incredibly encouraging. Hearing how others have trusted in God's promises and witnessed miraculous outcomes can bolster our faith and remind us that we are not alone in our journey. These stories serve as living proof that God is still at work, fulfilling His promises in remarkable ways. Whether it's a story of healing, financial provision, or relational restoration, these testimonies highlight the transformative power of God's promises when we choose to believe and trust in Him wholeheartedly.

In conclusion, embracing and claiming God's promises requires a deep understanding of His Word, a consistent prayer life, patience, and an unwavering trust in His timing. By immersing ourselves in scripture, praying His promises, and drawing encouragement from the testimonies of others, we can confidently hold on to the hope we profess. As Hebrews 10:23 urges, "Let us hold unswervingly to the hope we profess, for he who promised is faithful." God's promises are sure, and as we stand firm in faith, we will undoubtedly witness His faithfulness unfold in our lives, bringing about miraculous outcomes and fulfilling His divine purposes for us.

Trusting in His Timing

Understanding the power of God and trusting in His timing is fundamental to our faith. The Bible is filled with examples of God's mighty power and the fulfillment of His promises, often after long periods of waiting. These stories encourage us to remain patient and steadfast, knowing that God's timing is perfect and His promises are sure.

One of the most striking demonstrations of God's power is found in the creation account in Genesis. By His word alone, God created the heavens and the earth, light and darkness, land and sea, and all living creatures. "In the beginning, God created the heavens and the earth" (Genesis 1:1). This incredible display of power reminds us that the God who created everything from nothing is fully capable of orchestrating the events of our lives according to His perfect plan.

Another powerful story is the parting of the Red Sea in Exodus 14. When the Israelites were trapped between the Red Sea and the pursuing Egyptian army, they cried out in fear. But God, through Moses, parted the waters, allowing the Israelites to cross on dry ground and escape their enemies. "The Lord will fight for you; you need only to be still" (Exodus 14:14). This miraculous event highlights God's power to deliver and protect His people, even in seemingly impossible situations.

The story of Joseph also illustrates the power of God and the importance of trusting in His timing. Sold into slavery by his brothers, Joseph endured many hardships, including false accusations and imprisonment. Yet, through it all, he remained faithful to God. In time, God elevated Joseph to a position of great power in Egypt, where he ultimately saved many lives during a severe famine. Joseph's journey, which spanned many years, teaches us that God's plans often unfold over long periods and that His timing is perfect. As Joseph later told his brothers, "You intended to harm me, but God intended it for good to accomplish what is now being done, the saving of many lives" (Genesis 50:20).

In the New Testament, we see God's power through the resurrection of Jesus Christ. After suffering and dying on the cross, Jesus was raised to life on the third day, conquering sin and death. "But God raised him from the dead, freeing him from the agony of death, because it was impossible for death to keep its hold on him" (Acts 2:24). The resurrection is the ultimate demonstration of God's power and His faithfulness to fulfill His promises.

Trusting in God's timing can be challenging, especially when we face long periods of waiting or difficult circumstances. However, scripture reassures us that God's timing is perfect and that His promises will come to pass. "The Lord is not slow in keeping his promise, as some understand slowness. Instead, he is patient with you, not wanting anyone to perish, but everyone to come to repentance" (2 Peter 3:9). Additionally, Isaiah 40:31 encourages us, "But those who hope in the Lord will renew their strength. They will soar on wings like eagles; they will run and not grow weary; they will walk and not be faint."

In our own lives, we can draw strength from these biblical examples and trust that God's power is at work in every situation. We are encouraged to remain patient and steadfast, knowing that His promises are sure and will come to pass, no matter how long the wait. By relying on God's power and trusting in His timing, we can navigate life's challenges with hope and confidence.

Reflection and Application: Trusting in the Powers of God

Understanding God's Power

Thought-Provoking Questions:

1. How does the creation story in Genesis demonstrate God's power?
2. What can we learn about God's power from the parting of the Red Sea in Exodus 14?
3. How do these stories reinforce your faith in God's ability to orchestrate the events of your life?

Journal Prompts:

1. Reflect on a moment in your life where you experienced God's power firsthand. How did it strengthen your faith?
2. Write about a situation where you need to trust in God's power. How do the creation and the Red Sea stories inspire you in this situation?
3. Journal a prayer thanking God for His mighty power and asking for faith to trust in His plans for your life.

Trusting in God's Timing

Thought-Provoking Questions:

1. How did Joseph's long journey from slavery to a position of power demonstrate the importance of trusting in God's timing?
2. In what ways does the story of Joseph encourage you to remain patient during difficult times?
3. How does the resurrection of Jesus Christ reassure you of God's faithfulness to fulfill His promises?

Journal Prompts:

1. Reflect on a time when you had to wait for God's timing. What did you learn during that period?
2. Write about a current situation where you are waiting for God to move. How can you draw encouragement from Joseph's story?
3. Journal a prayer asking God for patience and trust in His perfect timing, especially in the areas where you are waiting for His promises to be fulfilled.

Dealing with Doubt and Discouragement

Thought-Provoking Questions:

1. What are some common reasons people struggle with trusting in God's timing?
2. How can scriptures like 2 Peter 3:9 and Isaiah 40:31 help you combat doubt and discouragement?
3. How can you encourage others who are struggling to trust in God's power and timing?

Journal Prompts:

1. Think about a time when you felt doubt or discouragement. How did you overcome it, or how are you working through it now?

2. Write about the promises of God that you are holding onto. How can you remind yourself of these promises during challenging times?

3. Journal a prayer for someone you know who is struggling with doubt or waiting on God's timing. Ask God to strengthen their faith and provide them with encouragement.

Applying Trust in Everyday Life

Thought-Provoking Questions:

1. How can you actively practice trusting in God's power and timing in your daily life?

2. What are some practical steps you can take to remain patient and faithful during periods of waiting?

3. How can you incorporate the lessons from these biblical stories into your own faith journey?

Journal Prompts:

1. Reflect on how you can make trusting in God's power and timing a daily practice. What changes do you need to make in your routine or mindset?

2. Write about a specific goal or dream you have. How can you trust God's timing and power to bring it to fruition?

3. Journal a prayer of commitment to trust in God's power and timing, asking for His guidance and strength as you navigate your journey of faith.

Chapter 8: Faith in Action

Living out our faith daily is essential to our spiritual growth. James 2:17 states, "In the same way, faith by itself, if it is not accompanied by action, is dead." This chapter offers practical ways to demonstrate faith in everyday life, encouraging you to be an active witness of God's love. Inspiring stories of faith in action will motivate readers to make a positive impact in their communities. Matthew 5:16 instructs, "In the same way, let your light shine before others, that they may see your good deeds and glorify your Father in heaven." By providing practical tips and real-life applications, this chapter empowers you to live boldly in your faith and be a light to those around you. Galatians 5:6 emphasizes, "For in Christ Jesus neither circumcision nor uncircumcision has any value. The only thing that counts is faith expressing itself through love."

Living Out Our Faith Daily

Living out our faith daily is essential to our spiritual growth and is a testament to our commitment to follow Christ. True faith is more than just belief; it is demonstrated through our actions, decisions, and interactions with others. James 2:17 says, "In the same way, faith by itself, if it is not accompanied by action, is dead." This scripture emphasizes that faith without deeds is incomplete. Our actions serve as evidence of our faith, revealing the transformation that has taken place within us.

Jesus taught the importance of faith in action through various parables and teachings. In the Parable of the Good Samaritan (Luke 10:25-37), Jesus illustrates what it means to love our neighbor. The Samaritan's actions, in contrast to the priest and Levite who passed by, demonstrate true compassion and mercy. This parable teaches us that living out our faith involves actively showing love and kindness to those in need, regardless of their background or circumstances. By prioritizing compassion over prejudice, the Samaritan exemplifies the heart of Jesus' teachings, urging us to embrace a lifestyle of active love and mercy.

Another powerful example is found in Matthew 25:31-46, where Jesus speaks about the final judgment. He distinguishes between the righteous and the unrighteous based on their actions, saying, "For I was hungry and you gave me something to eat, I was thirsty and you gave me something to drink, I was a stranger and you invited me in, I needed clothes and you clothed me, I was sick and you looked after me, I was in prison and you came to visit me." These acts of service and compassion are direct expressions of our faith and love for Christ. This passage highlights that our treatment of others, particularly the marginalized and needy, reflects our relationship with Jesus. By serving others, we serve Christ himself.

The Apostle Paul also emphasizes the importance of living out our faith in Galatians 5:6, "The only thing that counts is faith expressing itself through love." Paul encourages believers to let their faith be evident through acts of love, which fulfill the law of Christ. He further instructs in Colossians 3:17, "And whatever you do, whether in word or deed, do it all in the name of the Lord Jesus, giving thanks to God the Father through him." This verse underscores that every aspect of our lives should reflect our faith and bring glory to God. Whether we are at work, at home, or in our communities, our actions should be consistent with our faith, demonstrating integrity, kindness, and a commitment to God's glory.

Living out our faith daily involves practical steps such as prayer, reading and applying Scripture, serving others, and fostering a community of believers. It requires intentionality and commitment to align our actions with the teachings of Christ. By engaging in regular prayer, we maintain an open line of communication with God, seeking His guidance and strength. Reading and applying Scripture helps us to understand God's will and equips us to live according to His principles. Serving others, whether through small acts of kindness or more significant commitments, allows us to embody the love of Christ in tangible ways. Finally, fostering a community of believers provides support, accountability, and encouragement as we journey together in faith.

By doing so, we grow spiritually, strengthen our relationship with God, and become effective witnesses of His love and grace to the world. When our faith permeates our daily lives, it not only transforms us but also has the power to impact those around us. Our actions become a testament to God's work in us, drawing others to Him and glorifying His name.

Reflection and Application: Faith in Action

Understanding Faith in Action

Thought-Provoking Questions:

1. What does James 2:17 mean when it says faith without deeds is dead?
2. How does the Parable of the Good Samaritan illustrate the concept of faith in action?
3. In what ways do Jesus' teachings in Matthew 25:31-46 challenge you to live out your faith more fully?

Journal Prompts:

1. Reflect on a time when you put your faith into action. What did you do, and how did it impact you and others?
2. Write about an area in your life where you feel challenged to live out your faith more intentionally. How can you take practical steps to address this?
3. Journal a prayer asking God to help you demonstrate your faith through actions that reflect His love and compassion.

Serving Others

Thought-Provoking Questions:

1. How does serving others demonstrate our faith in Christ?
2. What practical ways can you serve those in need in your community or church?
3. How can you overcome obstacles that might prevent you from serving others effectively?

Journal Prompts:

1. Think about a person or group in need that you feel called to serve. Write about how you can make a difference in their lives through specific actions.
2. Reflect on a past experience of serving others. How did it strengthen your faith and spiritual growth?
3. Journal a commitment to serve others in a particular way this week. Describe what you will do and how you hope it will reflect your faith.

Expressing Love through Actions

Thought-Provoking Questions:

1. According to Galatians 5:6, how is faith expressed through love?
2. What are some everyday actions that can reflect Christ's love to those around you?
3. How can you cultivate a lifestyle that consistently expresses faith through love?

Journal Prompts:

1. Reflect on the concept of faith expressing itself through love. Write about how you can apply this principle in your relationships with family, friends, and colleagues.
2. Think of a recent situation where you had the opportunity to show love but didn't. How can you respond differently next time?
3. Journal a prayer asking God to fill your heart with His love and to help you express that love through your actions daily.

Aligning Actions with Faith

Thought-Provoking Questions:

1. How does Colossians 3:17 guide us in aligning our actions with our faith?
2. What areas of your life need more alignment with the teachings of Christ?
3. How can you ensure that your words and deeds consistently reflect your faith in Jesus?

Journal Prompts:

1. Reflect on your daily routine and activities. Are there any areas where your actions do not align with your faith? How can you change that?
2. Write about a specific teaching of Christ that you find challenging to live out. What steps can you take to better align your actions with this teaching?
3. Journal a prayer of dedication, asking God to help you live a life that reflects your faith in all that you do, bringing glory to Him.

Chapter 9: The Reward of Faithfulness

Remaining faithful to God brings incredible rewards. Matthew 25:21 records, "His master replied, 'Well done, good and faithful servant! You have been faithful with a few things; I will put you in charge of many things. Come and share your master's happiness!'" This chapter explores the blessings and breakthroughs that come from a life of faithfulness. Through testimonials of individuals who have experienced God's blessings, readers will be encouraged to persevere to the end. Hebrews 11:6 explains, "And without faith it is impossible to please God, because anyone who comes to him must believe that he exists and that he rewards those who earnestly seek him." Understanding the eternal significance of their faithfulness will inspire you to stay committed to God's call, knowing that their efforts are not in vain and that God rewards those who diligently seek Him. Revelation 2:10 promises, "Do not be afraid of what you are about to suffer. I tell you, the devil will put some of you in prison to test you, and you will suffer persecution for ten days. Be faithful, even to the point of death, and I will give you life as your victor's crown."

Faithfulness in the small things often precedes greater responsibilities and blessings. The parable of the talents (Matthew 25:14-30) illustrates how God honors those who are faithful with what they have been given. The servant who diligently invested his master's money was rewarded with increased responsibility and joy. This principle applies to every area of our lives; when we are faithful in our work, relationships, and spiritual disciplines, we open ourselves up to greater opportunities and blessings from God. Small acts of faithfulness, like consistent prayer, studying the Bible, or serving others, build a foundation for larger acts of faith. Over time, these small acts accumulate, leading to significant spiritual growth and deeper intimacy with God.

Moreover, remaining faithful often involves enduring hardships and persevering through trials. The book of James reminds us that the testing of our faith produces perseverance, leading to maturity and completeness (James 1:2-4). Many biblical figures, such as Job, Joseph, and Paul, faced significant trials but remained steadfast in their faith. Their stories demonstrate that God is with us in our struggles and that our perseverance will be rewarded. Joseph, for example, endured betrayal, slavery, and imprisonment but remained faithful to God. His faithfulness ultimately led to his rise to power in Egypt, where he was able to save many lives during a famine. Similarly, Paul's relentless faith, even in the face of persecution, allowed him to spread the Gospel and establish numerous churches. These examples inspire us to remain faithful, trusting that God has a purpose for our trials and that He will bring about His good plans in His timing.

In summary, remaining faithful to God not only brings rewards in this life but also has eternal significance. As we stay committed to God's call, we experience His blessings, grow spiritually, and make a lasting impact on those around us. Our faithfulness is a testament to our trust in God's promises and His faithfulness to us. By sharing testimonials of individuals who have experienced God's blessings through their faithfulness, this chapter encourages readers to persevere, knowing that their efforts are not in vain and that God rewards those who earnestly seek Him. Let us remain steadfast, even in the face of challenges, trusting that God is with us and that He will honor our faithfulness.

Remaining Faithful to God Brings Incredible Rewards

Remaining faithful to God, especially during challenging times, is a cornerstone of a strong and growing spiritual life. The Bible is replete with promises and examples that highlight the rewards of steadfast faith. From the Old Testament to the New Testament, the theme of God's faithfulness to those who remain true to Him is evident and deeply encouraging.

One of the most profound examples of faithfulness is Abraham. God promised Abraham that he would become the father of many nations, even though he and his wife Sarah were old and childless. Abraham's faith was tested over many years, but he remained faithful, trusting in God's promise. In Genesis 22, Abraham's willingness to sacrifice his son Isaac at God's command demonstrated his unwavering faith. God rewarded Abraham's faithfulness, saying, "I swear by myself, declares the Lord, that because you have done this and have not withheld your son, your only son, I will surely bless you and make your descendants as numerous as the stars in the sky and as the sand on the seashore" (Genesis 22:16-17).

Job is another exemplary figure of faithfulness in the Bible. Despite losing his wealth, health, and children, Job remained steadfast in his faith. He refused to curse God and instead continued to trust Him. In the end, God restored Job's fortunes and blessed him with twice as much as he had before. Job 42:10 states, "After Job had prayed for his friends, the Lord restored his fortunes and gave him twice as much as he had before." Job's story shows that unwavering faith, even in the face of immense suffering, brings incredible rewards.

In the New Testament, the Apostle Paul frequently speaks about the rewards of remaining faithful to God. In 2 Timothy 4:7-8, Paul reflects on his life and ministry, saying, "I have fought the good fight, I have finished the race, I have kept the faith. Now there is in store for me the crown of righteousness, which the Lord, the righteous Judge, will award to me on that day—and not only to me, but also to all who have longed for his appearing." Paul's assurance of eternal rewards for those who remain faithful is a powerful encouragement for all believers.

Jesus Himself emphasized the rewards of faithfulness in His teachings. In the Parable of the Talents (Matthew 25:14-30), Jesus illustrates that those who are faithful with what they have been given will be entrusted with more. The master in the parable says to the faithful servant, "Well done, good and faithful servant! You have been faithful with a few things; I will put you in charge of many things. Come and share your master's happiness" (Matthew 25:21). This parable highlights that faithfulness leads to greater responsibilities and joy in God's kingdom.

Remaining faithful to God also brings spiritual rewards such as peace, joy, and strength. Philippians 4:6-7 encourages believers, "Do not be anxious about anything, but in every situation, by prayer and petition, with thanksgiving, present your requests to God. And the peace of God, which transcends all understanding, will guard your hearts and your minds in Christ Jesus." Additionally, James 1:12 promises, "Blessed is the one who perseveres under trial because, having stood the test, that person will receive the crown of life that the Lord has promised to those who love him."

In summary, remaining faithful to God brings incredible rewards, both in this life and in eternity. By looking to biblical examples and promises, we can find the encouragement and strength to stay faithful, knowing that God is always faithful to us.

Reflection and Application: Remaining Faithful to God

Understanding Faithfulness

Thought-Provoking Questions:

1. How did Abraham's faithfulness to God bring incredible rewards to his life and his descendants?

2. In what ways did Job demonstrate unwavering faith, and what rewards did he receive from God?

3. How does Paul's reflection on his life and ministry in 2 Timothy 4:7-8 encourage you to remain faithful?

Journal Prompts:

1. Reflect on a time when you faced a significant test of faith. How did you respond, and what did you learn from that experience?

2. Write about an area in your life where you need to trust God more fully. How can you demonstrate faithfulness in this area?

3. Journal a prayer asking God for the strength and perseverance to remain faithful, especially during challenging times.

Biblical Examples of Faithfulness

Thought-Provoking Questions:

1. What lessons can you learn from the Parable of the Talents about faithfulness and stewardship?

2. How does Jesus' teaching on faithfulness in small things apply to your everyday life?

3. In what ways do the stories of Abraham, Job, and Paul inspire you to be more faithful in your own walk with God?

Journal Prompts:

1. Reflect on a specific biblical story of faithfulness that resonates with you. Write about how this story encourages you to trust God more deeply.

2. Think about the talents and resources God has entrusted to you. How can you be more faithful in using them for His glory?

3. Journal a prayer of thanksgiving for the examples of faithfulness in the Bible and ask God to help you apply these lessons to your life.

Spiritual Rewards of Faithfulness

Thought-Provoking Questions:

1. How does Philippians 4:6-7 describe the spiritual rewards of remaining faithful to God?

2. What does James 1:12 promise to those who persevere under trial?

3. How can you experience the peace and joy that come from remaining faithful to God, even in difficult circumstances?

Journal Prompts:

1. Reflect on a time when you experienced God's peace in the midst of a challenging situation. How did your faith play a role in that experience?

2. Write about a current trial you are facing. How can you remain faithful and trust in God's promises during this time?

3. Journal a prayer asking for God's peace, joy, and strength as you strive to remain faithful in all aspects of your life.

Applying Faithfulness in Daily Life

Thought-Provoking Questions:

1. How can you practice faithfulness in your daily routines and responsibilities?

2. What are some practical steps you can take to grow in faithfulness to God?

3. How can you encourage others in their journey of faithfulness to God

Journal Prompts:

1. Reflect on your daily routine. Are there areas where you need to be more faithful to God? How can you make changes to better align with His will?

2. Write about a person or group you feel called to encourage in their faith journey. How can you support and uplift them?

3. Journal a prayer of dedication, asking God to help you live a life of faithfulness in all that you do, trusting in His promises and rewards.

Conclusion

Faith is about believing in God's promises and acting on them, despite what our circumstances may look like. This book serves as a powerful reminder that God's word is true, His promises are sure, and His presence is constant. Throughout the pages of this book, we have explored the essence of faith and the importance of remaining steadfast, even when life seems uncertain and challenging. Hebrews 13:5 assures us, "Never will I leave you; never will I forsake you." This profound promise from God is a cornerstone of our faith, providing comfort and strength in times of trouble. It reassures us that we are never alone; God is always with us, guiding and sustaining us through every storm.

As we navigate the journey of faith, it is crucial to remember that our circumstances do not define God's faithfulness. The trials we face are opportunities to deepen our trust in Him and to witness His power at work in our lives. Psalm 119:105 tells us, "Your word is a lamp for my feet, a light on my path." God's word provides the guidance and clarity we need to walk through life's darkest moments. It illuminates our path, helping us to make decisions that align with His will and to move forward with confidence, knowing that He is leading the way.

The stories and teachings within this book have highlighted the lives of individuals who remained faithful to God despite overwhelming odds. Their examples inspire us to trust in God's promises and to act on them, regardless of the challenges we face. Faith is not a passive belief but an active trust that compels us to live out God's word in every aspect of our lives. It requires us to stand firm, to be courageous, and to draw strength from the assurance that God is with us.

1 Corinthians 16:13 exhorts us, "Be on your guard; stand firm in the faith; be courageous; be strong." This call to action is a powerful reminder of the resilience and determination required to live a life of faith. It encourages us to remain vigilant, to protect our hearts and minds from doubt and fear, and to stand firm in the promises of God. Courage and strength are essential qualities for a believer, enabling us to face challenges head-on and to overcome them with God's help.

As you reflect on the lessons and insights from this book, I encourage you to apply them to your daily life. Allow God's word to shape your thoughts, actions, and decisions. Embrace the promises He has made to you and trust in His perfect timing. Remember that faith is a journey, not a destination. It is a continuous process of growing closer to God, of learning to rely on Him more deeply, and of witnessing His faithfulness in every situation.

The central message of this book is to keep the faith and to believe what God has said, regardless of the challenges faced. Faith anchors us in God's truth, providing stability and hope in the midst of life's storms. It empowers us to rise above our circumstances and to see God's hand at work, even when the way forward seems unclear. By standing firm in our faith, we open ourselves to the incredible rewards that come from a deep and abiding trust in God.

In conclusion, let the words of Hebrews 13:5, Psalm 119:105, and 1 Corinthians 16:13 resonate in your heart. Let them remind you of God's unwavering presence, His guiding light, and the strength and courage He imparts to His faithful followers. May you continue to walk by faith, to stand firm on God's promises, and to trust in His unchanging word. No matter what challenges you face, know that God is with you every step of the way, leading you toward a future filled with His goodness and grace

Frequently Asked Questions

Q: What does it mean to "walk by faith, not by sight"?

A: Walking by faith means living with a confident trust in God's character and promises, even when circumstances appear uncertain or challenging. The Apostle Paul encourages believers, "For we walk by faith, not by sight" (2 Corinthians 5:7, ESV). This means relying on God's wisdom and guidance rather than solely on what we can perceive with our senses. It involves aligning our decisions and actions with God's Word and His revealed will, trusting that He is working all things together for our good and His glory (Romans 8:28).

Q: How can I strengthen my faith?

A: Strengthening faith is a lifelong journey that involves several key practices:

- **Prayer**: Regularly communicate with God, expressing your concerns, desires, and praises. Prayer deepens your relationship with Him and aligns your heart with His will (Philippians 4:6-7).
- **Studying God's Word**: Dive into Scripture daily to understand God's character, His promises, and His plan for your life. Meditate on His Word and apply it to your circumstances (Psalm 119:105).
- **Christian Community**: Surround yourself with fellow believers who can encourage, support, and pray for you. Iron sharpens iron, and being part of a supportive community strengthens your faith journey (Hebrews 10:24-25).
- **Stepping out in Obedience**: Actively obey God's commands and follow His leading in your life. Obedience demonstrates your trust in God's wisdom and faithfulness (James 1:22).
- **Reflecting on God's Faithfulness**: Recall and celebrate past instances where God has been faithful to you. Remembering His faithfulness in the past bolsters your confidence in His faithfulness for the future (Psalm 77:11-12).

Q: What do I do when my faith is tested?

A: Trials and challenges are opportunities for spiritual growth and refinement. When your faith is tested:

- **Turn to God in Prayer**: Bring your concerns and struggles to God in earnest prayer. He invites us to cast all our anxieties on Him because He cares for us (1 Peter 5:7).
- **Lean on Scripture**: Find comfort and strength in the promises of God's Word. Meditate on passages that remind you of His sovereignty, love, and provision (Isaiah 41:10).
- **Seek Support**: Don't face trials alone. Reach out to trusted Christian friends or mentors who can pray for you, provide wise counsel, and offer support (Galatians 6:2).

- **Trust in God's Purpose**: Remember that God uses trials to build perseverance, character, and hope in us. Trust that He has a purpose and a plan, even in the midst of difficulties (James 1:2-4).

Q: How do I know if I'm following God's will?

A: Discerning God's will requires seeking His guidance and aligning your desires and decisions with His Word and character:

- **Prayer and Seeking God's Guidance**: Spend time in prayer, asking God for wisdom and clarity regarding His will for your life (James 1:5).
- **Study Scripture**: Regularly read and meditate on God's Word. Scripture serves as a lamp to our feet and a light to our path, guiding us in making decisions that honor God (Psalm 119:105).
- **Peace and Confirmation**: Look for a sense of peace and confirmation from the Holy Spirit, as well as alignment with biblical principles and wise counsel from mature believers (Proverbs 11:14).

Q: What role does obedience play in walking by faith?

A: Obedience is an essential expression of faith. When we obey God's commands and follow His leading:

- **Demonstration of Trust**: Obedience demonstrates our trust in God's wisdom, goodness, and faithfulness. It shows that we believe His ways are higher and better than our own (Proverbs 3:5-6).
- **Alignment with God's Will**: Obedience aligns our actions with God's will, reflecting our desire to honor Him and bring glory to His name (John 14:23).
- **Blessings and Rewards**: God promises blessings and rewards for those who obey Him wholeheartedly. Obedience opens the door for God to work mightily in and through our lives (John 15:10-11).

Appendix: Additional Resources for Deepening Your Faith

In this appendix, you will find a curated list of resources to further enhance your understanding and practice of walking by faith:

1. *Recommended Reading*
   - Books on faith, trust in God, and biblical examples of faith.
2. *Scripture References*
   - Key Bible verses on faith and trusting in God's promises.
3. *Study Guides and Workbooks*
   - Practical tools to help you apply the principles of faith in your daily life.
4. *Online Resources*
   - Websites, podcasts, and articles that offer insights and teachings on faith.
5. *Discussion Questions*
   - Thought-provoking questions to facilitate group discussions or personal reflection on faith.

This appendix is designed to supplement the content of this book and assist you in deepening your journey of faith. Whether you are seeking further study, practical applications, or community engagement, these resources aim to support and encourage your growth in faith.

Milton Keynes UK
Ingram Content Group UK Ltd.
UKHW052043081124
450822UK00010B/147